"Stella t  y
careful a Me,
I stopped .... cups.
Stella kept goin' 'til she filled a whole book."

—Dolly Parton

"Stella's always been a great talent on the stage and
this book will prove she's a great talent in the
kitchen, too."

—Donna Fargo

"Stella's just got to be one of the best cooks in
Tennessee."

—Lacy J. Dalton

"Congratulations on your new cookbook. Having
authored four of my own, I appreciate the hours of
preparation you have devoted to the project and I
know it will be a collector's must-have."

—Jeanne Pruett

"A good recipe is like a good song. Once you taste it
you'll never forget it."

—Kitty Wells

"You've got Chef Boyardee beat by a country mile."
—Melba Montgomery

"You and me both come from large families and us
country girls flat know how to cook, don't we."

—Loretta Lynn

Stella Parton's
Country Cookin'

Stella Parton's Country Cookin'

*From Slum Gullion to Blushing Tuna Pie,
Cabbage Strudel to Mama's Fried Taters,
Mississippi Mud Cake to Willadeene's
Watermelon Punch,
Dolly's Dill Dumplings,
and Sin Pie*

ADAMS PUBLISHING
HOLBROOK, MASSACHUSETTS

Published by Adams Media Corporation
260 Center Street, Holbrook, MA 02343

ISBN: 1-55850-473-7

Printed in the United States of America.

J I H G F E D C B A

Library of Congress Cataloging-in-Publication Data
Parton, Stella
    Stella Parton's country cookin' / Stella Parton.
        p.   cm.
    Includes index.
    ISBN 1-55850-473-7
    1. Cookery, American. 2. Parton, Stella. I. Title.
TX715.P2992   1995
    641.5—dc20   95-5292
                                                   CIP

This book is available at quantity discounts for bulk purchases. For information, call 1-800-872-5627.

Contents

Preface

One of my sweetest memories of cooking is one summer when Mama was canning blackberry jelly and jam. I decided I would fill up little baby food jars from her batch and serve them to Daddy at dinner. He told Mom that my jellies were much better than hers although they came from the same kettle. I was convinced he was right. She allowed him to bestow these compliments on me, which encouraged my desire to become a good cook. Most of my friends and family think I am, which I appreciate.

Cooking is certainly one of my most treasured forms of sharing love and warmth with the people I care about. Even a finicky eater will be pleased if you go to a little extra trouble on their behalf. I know because I used to be finicky when I was young and my Mom and Dad would go a bit extra for me without making too big a fuss. I have never liked melon of any kind; in the summertime when everyone else was having a nice cold slice of watermelon on Sunday afternoon after church, Daddy would always sneak me a Hershey's chocolate bar.

Cooking in a country home such as the one I grew up in was never a complicated deal. If you have a good frying pan, a good stew kettle, a couple of good sharp knives, and a good stir spoon, you can make just about anything your heart desires. You don't even need a rolling pin except when you need to hit your husband. All you really need is a good smooth glass for rolling out dough for pie crust, biscuits and an occasional batch of cookies.

My sisters are all good cooks, but Cassie, Rachel, and Willadeene are the better bakers because they are more patient and can follow a recipe with a bit more discipline than Dolly or myself. We have a tendency to think if a little dab will do you, then a lot will really make it taste good. Therefore, we are better at stews, soups, and casseroles. But if we get it right, it's usually really good. Mom reports that my sister Freida is probably the most creative cook of her six daughters. We may eventually have a cooking contest and blindfold all the grandchildren for a taste test.

Cooking is such a great thing because everybody likes to eat. I like to cook so let's just see what we can get into here in this collection of recipes and family photos. While going through my pictures I realized that a large percentage of my photographs were taken at family celebrations centered around food and I believe that's how it is in most families. Variety is supposed to be the spice of life, but I think if you can have potatoes, tomatoes, onions, garlic, and real butter at each family feast then you can satisfy the taste buds of most of the Parton clan. Happy eating and make every family meal a celebration.

Acknowledgments

I would like to thank Kimberly Mason, Harold Newson, Angela Hornbeck, Charlotte M. Sellers, Jessie Clarence Brown, Desiree Verble, Kendall Kitchens, Bubba Edwards, Darryle Reece, Rhonda Stanley, Scott Eddins, Thelma Ricketts, Andy Woodward, Judy McCarrel, Janet Reed, Margrette McMillin, Cheryl Douglas, Thelma Gullett, Lisa Lee, Sue Messer, Mike Lynn, Ella Mae Cheesman, Ann Whitsett, Eleanor Dial, Brian Wallace, Margie Corker, Lisa Higginbotham, Gene and Adaline Echer, Joe Williams, Bob and Norene Teague, Kirk Winter, Sandy Stevens, Monica Holt, Opal Stevens, Kathy Smith, Helen Johnson, Tina Farmer, Sheri Malloy, Lillian Maddox, Valley Mae Russsell, Ken Harper, Carolyn Cross, Vickey Hendricks, Carolyn Hollaran, Melissa Hayes, Cheryl Dial, Vernell Hackett, Joyce Rice, Victory Institute, Mary Ellen Bosendahl, and Tammy McDonie. Special thanks to Judy McCarrel for all her help in collecting family recipes.

FAMILY
SPECIALTIES

Mama's Fried 'Taters

Mama makes the best fried 'taters in the world! I make Mama's Fried 'Taters on Christmas morning. We also make these at the Hat House. I've added Italian seasoning as a twist. Mama says it ain't necessary. I say, "Mama, everybody likes it."

6 medium potatoes
1 large chopped onion
1 diced red pepper
1 diced green pepper
$^1/_2$ cup safflower oil
salt and pepper

Peel potatoes and slice thin. Heat oil in a large skillet over medium heat. Add potatoes. Salt and pepper to taste. Put the lid on them and let steam like Mama does. Add onion, green and red pepper, and cook. Optional: add 1 tablespoon Italian seasoning.

Cas Walker, a 92-year-old grocer who is legendary for his promotion of country music, came to the Hat House in Pigeon Forge, Tennessee, to sing a couple of songs. Dolly and I made our first professional appearances on his show.

Mama's 'Tater Biscuits

2 eggs, beaten
1 small tomato, finely chopped (optional)
4 to 5 cups left-over mashed potatoes
1 small onion
1 tablespoon dry parsley
$^{1}/_{2}$ cup flour
salt and pepper

Mix all ingredients into a stiff batter in a large mixing bowl. Drop batter by heaping table-spoons into hot safflower oil (Mama still uses bacon grease) and fry until brown on both sides, turning once. Place on paper towel to soak up extra oil. Serve while still warm. Mama says you should always fry 'taters in an iron skillet.

A little pre-Christmas gift exchange. Girls' night out.

Mama's Gingerbread

This was not a weekly treat, but was made during the winter time on special occasions like Christmas. We were always surprised by how it turned out, but it was always delicious. Mama served it with homemade applesauce and lots of butter.

$^1/_2$ **cup sugar**
1 cup molasses
1-$^1/_2$ teaspoons ginger
$^1/_2$ **teaspoon cinnamon**
$^1/_2$ **cup butter**
2 cups flour, plain
$^1/_2$ **teaspoon baking soda**
$^1/_2$ **cup buttermilk**

Mix all ingredients in a large mixing bowl. Bake at 350 degrees in a slightly greased bread pan, 45 minutes or until done.

Emergency Cornmeal Mush

5 cups water
1-$^1/_2$ teaspoons salt
1 cup white or yellow cornmeal
butter
milk

Heat water in saucepan. Add cornmeal and salt. Use additional cornmeal if needed. Stir and boil slowly until mixture thickens. Serve warm with butter and milk on the top.

We always had cornmeal mush in the winter time when we ran out of groceries and couldn't go anywhere to buy food. I hated mush because it made me feel we were poor. I like it now. I make it on a snowy day when the roads are slippery and it's just too cold to go out.

Mom & Dad on their 55th anniversary.

Fried Green Tomatoes

All my family loves tomatoes. We were so eager to eat them we couldn't wait 'til they got ripe.

I have learned that fried green tomatoes are an acquired taste. I made them for a gentleman friend. He didn't appreciate them at all. Needless to say, I didn't cook for him again.

2 to 3 green tomatoes, sliced
salt to taste
$^1/_4$ cup safflower oil
dash of Parmesan cheese (optional)
2 eggs, beaten
1 cup flour

Mix salt, parmesan cheese, and egg mixture in a large mixing bowl. Dip tomato slices into mixture. Cover slices evenly with flour. Fry on medium heat in oil until golden brown on both sides.

Cassie's Casserole

2 cups green beans (frozen)
2 cups green lima beans (frozen)
2 cups green peas (frozen)

Cook each vegetable separately. When ready to serve, mix together.

Dressing mixture:

1 teaspoon mustard
1 teaspoon Worcestershire sauce
$1 \cdot {}^1/_2$ cups salad dressing or mayonnaise
3 hard boiled eggs (chopped)
1 medium onion (chopped fine)
1 tablespoon lemon juice
dash of garlic powder (to taste)
$^1/_4$ teaspoon Tabasco sauce (optional)

Mix dressing with hot vegetables when ready to serve.

Mom and Dad at home. My son Tim took this picture on a weekend visit. He and I try to visit my folks as often as possible.

8

Dolly's Dill Dumpling

We have these on the menu at the Hat House. Everybody loves them, especially when *I* make them, of course.

2 cups cholesterol-free Bisquick
1 cup milk
1 teaspoon dill
1 tablespoon sugar
$^1/_2$ stick butter

Mix together and drop by tablespoon into boiling stew such as: stewed tomatoes, potatoes, beef, or chicken. It doesn't matter, just whatever you want. Sprinkle a bit of dill on top of the dumplings. Cover and let cook about ten minutes on medium heat. Serve hot.

Freida's Fried Okra

1 pound fresh okra
$^1/_2$ cup flour
$^1/_2$ cup oatmeal
$^1/_2$ teaspoon salt
pepper to taste

Wash and dry okra on paper towel. Cut in good sized pieces. Mix flour, salt, pepper, and oatmeal together and coat okra in the flour mixture in a zip-lock or paper bag. Fry in hot oil 'til brown and crispy. Drain on paper towel. Serve while hot. I like it with mashed potatoes and sliced tomatoes.

Rachel's Rhubarb Pie

2 cups rhubarb,   **1-$^1/_4$ cups sugar**
      cut in small pieces   **1 tablespoon butter**

Melt butter in a sauce pan then add sugar and rhubarb. Mix well and cook ten minutes on medium heat. Then add:

2 tablespoons cornstarch   **2 egg yolks**
$^1/_2$ cup cream   **$^1/_8$ teaspoon salt**

Cook 'til thick, about fifteen minutes. Pour into a 9-inch baked pie shell. Top with meringue made from the two left-over egg whites and brown slightly. This is excellent!

Willadeene's Watermelon Punch

This can be served in watermelon half that has been scalloped with a sharp knife. I think Willadeene spikes this punch. She won't tell, but she and Daddy know how to make home-brew and home-made wine from blackberries. It can also be frozen and served as sherbet.

1 gallon watermelon juice
1 cup distilled water
2 cups white sugar
1 quart ginger ale
1 teaspoon red food coloring

Cut watermelon in half. Scoop out contents, mash and strain off watermelon juice, which should be about one gallon. Bring to a boil with the distilled water and sugar 'til dissolved. Add food coloring and mix together well, then chill. When ready to serve, add ginger ale.

For Dolly's Christmas special, Rachel did Dolly's make-up and I was the associate producer.

APPETIZERS

Hot Mandarin Cider

8 Mandarin Orange Spice tea bags
3 cups boiling water
2 tablespoons honey (or to taste)
3 cups apple cider

In large container, pour boiling water over tea bags and steep for 5 minutes. Remove tea bags. Add honey to hot tea. Stir in apple cider. Heat to serving temperature. Do not boil. Serves 6 to 8.

Mandarin Citrus Spice

8 Mandarin Orange Spice tea bags
2 cups boiling water
$^1/_4$ cup honey (or to taste)
1 cup grapefruit juice
2 cups orange juice
2 cups ice cubes
2 12-ounce cans lemon/lime soda

In large container pour boiling water over tea bags and steep for 5 minutes. Remove tea bags. Add honey to hot tea. Stir in juices, ice, and lemon/lime soda. Serve over ice. Serves 9 to 12.

Hummus
(Pita Bread Snack)

¹/₃ cup tahini
¹/₄ cup lemon juice
4 cloves garlic, minced
3–4 drops Tabasco sauce
¹/₄ cup liquid from garbanzo
    beans

¹/₂ teaspoon cumin
2 15-ounce cans garbanzo
    beans, drained (reserve
    some of the liquid)
1 tablespoon olive oil

Combine all ingredients in food processor or blender. Blend to creamy paste. If too thick, add a little of the reserved liquid from the garbanzo beans.

Most of these ingredients can be bought in markets that sell ethnic produce.

Roquefort Dressing

1 pound Roquefort cheese (crumbled)
1 pint mayonnaise
1 clove garlic (finely chopped)
1 can evaporated milk
juice of one lemon

Mix all ingredients well and store in refrigerator. Will keep well. Makes about one quart.

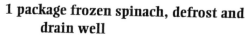

Spinach Dip

1 package frozen spinach, defrost and
    drain well
2 tablespoons parsley
3 green onions (chopped)
2 tablespoons chives (chopped)
1 bunch watercress (leaves only)
1 teaspoon Dijon mustard
2 teaspoons dill weed
2 teaspoons tarragon
2 teaspoons basil
1 teaspoon anchovy paste
2 cups mayonnaise
1 cup sour cream
2 tablespoons lemon juice
dash Tabasco sauce
pepper to taste

Blend all ingredients except spinach in
blender. Add spinach, blend 10 seconds, and
season to taste. This may be made up to three
weeks in advance. It is also delicious on fish.
Makes 4 cups.

*Jada, Timmy, Danielle, me, and
Clint at another family food fest.*

Party Rye Pizzas

1 pound grated Swiss cheese
1 bunch green onions (tops too), chopped finely
1 pound bacon, fried crisp and crumbled

Mix all ingredients with a little mayonnaise and spread on Party Rye bread.
Place on pizza pan and heat until cheese melts at 325 degrees. Serve hot.

Cream Cheese Spread

1 8-ounce package cream cheese
$^1/_2$ bottle Lemets chili sauce
1 teaspoon Worcestershire sauce
1 medium clove of garlic (mashed)
$^1/_2$ cup chopped olives, finely chopped

Soften cream cheese and mix all ingredients. Chill until ready to serve.

Stuffed Olives

25 green pitted jumbo olives
2–3 teaspoons finely minced onion
4 ounces shredded sharp Cheddar cheese
$^1/_2$ cup all purpose flour
$^1/_4$ teaspoon salt
$^1/_8$ teaspoon dry mustard
3 tablespoons melted
     and cooled margarine
1 teaspoon milk
2 drops Tabasco sauce

Mix flour, margarine, cheese, salt, mustard, onion, Tabasco sauce, and milk. Wrap this mixture around the olives and bake at 400 degrees. Cool and serve.

The boys in the band and me at the Jimmie Rodgers Festival in Meridian, Mississippi

Sausage Balls

1 pound sausage, hot or mild
2 cups biscuit mix

Mix together and shape into balls. Fry.

You can also do this same thing with Soyage* patties instead of the real thing. Add 2 tablespoons of vegetable oil.

These can also be baked to reduce the fat.

*Protein product seasoned with sage and found in health food sections.

Party Cheese Ball

$^1/_2$ cup chopped walnuts
3–5 ounces blue cheese
1 8-ounce package cream cheese
$^1/_4$ teaspoon garlic salt
1 tablespoon chopped green pepper
1 tablespoon chopped pimento

Spread walnuts in a shallow pan and toast for 8-10 minutes at 350 degrees, stirring occasionally until golden brown. Blend cheeses, garlic salt, pimento, and green pepper. Roll cheese mixture in toasted walnuts. Chill until firm.

Curried Liver Spread

8 ounces chicken livers
1 tablespoon butter or margarine
2 hard boiled eggs, halved
1 small onion, halved
$^1/_4$ cup mayonnaise or salad dressing
1 tablespoon lemon juice
1 tablespoon curry powder
$^1/_2$ tablespoon paprika
$^1/_4$ tablespoon salt
dash of pepper
$^1/_4$ teaspoon dry mustard
1 tablespoon finely chopped parsley
crackers or party bread rounds

In small skillet, brown chicken livers in butter or margarine. Put chicken livers, eggs, and onion through fine blade of food grinder or puree in a blender or food processor. Blend in mayonnaise, lemon juice, curry powder, paprika, salt, pepper, and mustard. Line a small bowl with clear plastic wrap. Spoon liver mixture into bowl, and cover. Chill. Unmold onto serving dish. Serve with crackers. Makes 1-$^3/_4$ cups of spread. Sprinkle parsley on top for serving.

Doing my patriotic duty, entertaining the returning troops from Desert Storm at Ft. Campbell, Kentucky.

Cheesy
Wheat Germ Spread

1 cup shredded Cheddar cheese (4 ounces)
$^1/_3$ cup mayonnaise or salad dressing
1 teaspoon lemon juice
1 teaspoon Worcestershire sauce
$^1/_2$ cup finely chopped apple
$^1/_2$ cup finely shredded carrot
$^1/_4$ cup finely chopped celery
$^1/_4$ cup chopped walnuts
2 tablespoons finely chopped
      green pepper
1 tablespoon wheat germ
$^1/_2$ cup raisins

Have cheese at room temperature. In small
mixing bowl, combine cheese, mayonnaise or
salad dressing, lemon juice, and Worcestershire
sauce. Beat 'til nearly smooth. Fold in apple,
carrot, celery, walnuts, raisins, green pepper,
and wheat germ. Cover and chill. Stir to blend
ingredients before serving. Serve on whole
wheat or rye bread. Makes 2 cups of spread.

Moss Ball

1 8-ounce package cream cheese
$^1/_4$–$^1/_2$ pound blue cheese (crumbled)
1 pound sharp Cheddar cheese (grated)
1 small onion (minced)
1 tablespoon Worcestershire sauce
$^1/_2$ cup chopped pecans
finely chopped parsley

Place cheeses in mixer bowl and let stand at room temperature until softened. Beat on medium speed until well mixed. Add onion and Worcestershire sauce and beat well. Stir in pecans. Chill 3 to 4 hours. Roll mixture into large ball. Chill and roll in parsley. Put on serving plate. Chill 2 hours or until firm. Serve with a variety of crackers. (May be divided into 2 balls.)

Aunt Ella's Cheese Ball

2 8-ounce packages cream cheese
1 8-ounce package sharp Cheddar cheese
1 green onion, chopped
1 teaspoon lemon juice
$^1/_2$ of a small jar of pimento
dash of Worcestershire sauce
1 cup chopped nuts

Mix ingredients together. Chill to firm. Roll in chopped nuts. Serve with favorite snack crackers.

Party Cheese Ball

2 8-ounce packages cream cheese
2 4-ounce packages sharp Cheddar
    cheese (grated)
1 tablespoon chopped pimento
1 tablespoon finely chopped green onion
1 teaspoon Worcestershire sauce
1 teaspoon lemon juice
dash of cayenne and salt

Combine softened ingredients (cream cheese
and Cheddar cheese) mixing until blended.
Add pimento, green onion, Worcestershire
sauce, lemon juice, and seasonings. Mix well.
Chill. Shape into a ball and roll in finely
chopped parsley.

*A wine cellar in Bazel,
Switzerland. What a way to
spend a day.*

Liverwurst Paté

1 pound liverwurst, mashed with fork
1 clove garlic, pressed
$^1/_2$ teaspoon sweet basil
3 tablespoons minced onion
Cream Cheese Topping (below)

Blend first 4 ingredients thoroughly. Shape into igloo shape on serving plate. Chill while making topping.

Cream Cheese Topping

Mix:

1 8-ounce package cream cheese
1 clove garlic, pressed
$^1/_8$ teaspoon Tabasco sauce
1 teaspoon mayonnaise

Spread topping over liverwurst. Spread with caviar (if desired). Chill overnight. Serve with crackers.

To give an igloo look: spread cream cheese topping over igloo shape, then use a toothpick to score the cream to resemble the blocks of ice of an igloo.

BREADS

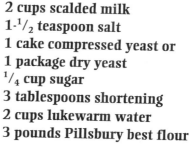

Pillsbury Yeast Bread

2 cups scalded milk
1-$^1/_2$ teaspoon salt
1 cake compressed yeast or
1 package dry yeast
$^1/_4$ cup sugar
3 tablespoons shortening
2 cups lukewarm water
3 pounds Pillsbury best flour

Combine scalded milk, sugar, salt and shorten-ing. Stir until dissolved and lukewarm. Soften yeast in $^1/_2$ cup lukewarm water. Add yeast and remaining water to cooled milk mixture. Sift flour once, then measure. Add $^1/_2$ the flour to yeast mixture. Beat well. Add rest of flour and blend well. Knead on floured board for 10 minutes. Place in greased bowl and cover. Let rise in warm place 80 to 85 minutes until impression of finger stays in dough. Punch gas from dough, cover, and let rise again for about 30 minutes. Make into 3 balls, let rise closely covered 15 minutes. Shape into loaves. Place in greased 9 x 5 x 3 inch loaf pans. Cover and let rise until doubled and center rises above the top, about 2 hours. Preheat oven to 450 degrees for 10 minutes. Reduce heat to 350 degrees. Bake 40 minutes. Remove loaves from pans and cool on racks.

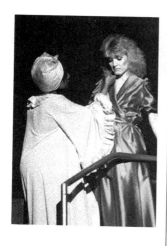

Andrei Karen-Anderson and me in a scene from "Best Little Whorehouse" tour.

Quick Rising Sweet Dough

$^3/_4$ cup milk (whole)
1-$^1/_2$ teaspoons salt
$^3/_4$ cup very warm water
5-$^1/_2$ cups unsifted flour
$^1/_2$ cup sugar
1 stick margarine
3 packages dry yeast

In saucepan, scald milk. In a small bowl, dissolve the yeast in $^1/_4$-cup water (lukewarm). Put margarine, sugar, and salt in large bowl. Pour the scalded milk and water over this. Cool to lukewarm. Add the yeast. Mix well. Add flour and mix smooth. Let rise double, punch down, and roll to make Parker House Clover Leaf or whatever. Put in greased pans and let rise and bake at 400 degrees, 12 to 14 minutes or until done.

This is for Parker House rolls or rolls of this type.

Dolly and Tim at Tim's 21st birthday party. We try not to have too much fun.

30

Buttermilk Biscuits

2 cups flour
1 tablespoon baking powder
1 cup buttermilk
$^3/_4$ teaspoon salt
$^1/_4$ cup shortening
$^1/_4$ teaspoon baking soda

In a large bowl, mix dry ingredients with shortening, to pie crust consistency, and add buttermilk. Cut out biscuits and bake in 450 degree oven 15 minutes.

Buttermilk Cheese Bread

2 cups flour
$^1/_2$ teaspoon baking soda
1 teaspoon salt
1 cup buttermilk
1-$^1/_2$ teaspoons baking powder

2 teaspoons dry mustard
1 cup Cheddar cheese (shredded)
$^1/_4$ cup oil
2 eggs

In large bowl, combine flour, baking powder, soda, mustard, salt, and cheese. Set aside. In another bowl, beat eggs, oil, and buttermilk with rotary beater until blended. Add all at once to flour mixture and mix just until moist. Pour into greased 9 x 5 x 3 inch pan and bake at 375 degrees about 45 minutes or until pick comes out clean. Cool in pan 10 minutes, invert on rack, and cool.

Herbed Monkey Bread

$^1/_2$ cup butter
2 teaspoons parsley, minced
$^1/_2$ teaspoon basil
2 cloves garlic, minced
1 green onion, minced
2 8-ounce packages Pillsbury Butter Flake Dinner Rolls

Melt butter in saucepan. Add herbs and onions. Pour 2 tablespoons butter around mold to grease. Dip each roll in herb batter. Place staggered fashion in bundt or angel food pan. Place in oven for 20 minutes at 350 to 375 degrees until brown.

Date Tea Bread

1 8-ounce package dates	1-$^1/_4$ cups boiling water
1-$^1/_2$ cups packed brown sugar	6 tablespoons butter
1 egg, beaten	2-$^1/_4$ cups flour
1-$^1/_2$ teaspoons baking powder	1-$^1/_2$ teaspoons salt

Cut up dates into a medium sized bowl. Pour boiling water over the dates. Stir in sugar and butter until butter melts. Cool. Stir in beaten egg. Mix flour, baking powder, and salt. Stir into date mixture just until blended. Pour into greased 9 x 5 x 3 inch loaf pan. Let stand 15 minutes. Bake 350 degrees 1 hour 10 minutes or until toothpick comes out clean. Cool in pan 5 minutes. Turn out on wire rack to cool. Store at least 1 day before cutting.

Stella Parton's Country Cookin'

Banana Nut Bread

3 ripe bananas, mashed
2 cups flour
2 eggs slightly beaten
$^1/_2$ cup butter or margarine
1 cup white sugar

1 teaspoon baking soda
1 teaspoon vanilla
1 cup nuts, chopped
$^1/_2$ teaspoon salt

In a large mixing bowl, cream together shortening and sugar. Add eggs and vanilla. Add flour, salt, and soda. Add bananas and nuts. Pour into greased and floured pans. Bake 350 degrees 35 to 40 minutes.

Black Walnut Loaf

1 cup sugar
1 egg
pinch of salt
1-$^1/_2$ cups flour
$^1/_2$ pint sour cream
1 cup black walnuts, chopped

In a large bowl, mix all ingredients. Pour batter into lightly buttered loaf pan. Bake one hour at 350 degrees.

Angel Biscuits

3 cups flour
3 tablespoons sugar
1-$^1/_2$ teaspoons baking powder
$^1/_2$ teaspoon baking soda
$^1/_2$ teaspoon salt
$^1/_2$ cup shortening
1 package dry yeast (dissolved in 2 tablespoons warm water)
1 cup buttermilk

Sift dry ingredients together. Add dissolved
yeast to buttermilk. Work shortening into
flour mixture. Add buttermilk and mix well
like biscuit dough. Put out onto floured board
or towel and roll to $^1/_4$ inch thickness. Cut
with biscuit cutter. Spread with melted butter.
Fold over for pocket book rolls. Bake until
lightly browned.

This recipe was
given to Helen by
her neighbor, Mrs.
Ford. It's very good.

*My sisters, Cassie and Rachel, at
my surprise birthday party.
Obviously, I'm the one in the
middle without make-up. What
a great surprise!*

Whole Wheat Bread

This recipe for bread dates back to Steve's college days at Indiana University. I left the wording as it was given to him by his sister Judy.

2 cups milk
2 teaspoons salt
2 tablespoons honey
2 tablespoons unsulphured molasses
$^1/_2$ teaspoon sugar
1 package active dry yeast
2 tablespoons butter
4-$^2/_3$ cups whole wheat flour
4 tablespoons warm water

Do sugar, yeast, water in a cup. Let fizzle 15 minutes. In a big bowl, pour milk, salt, honey, molasses, and butter. When yeast is done pour into milk mixture. Stir well. Dump all of this into the flour. Stir until moistened. Scrape down sides of bowl. Cover with towel (old rug, blanket, etc.) and let rise 1 hour. It will look the same, but feel differently. Knead 10–15 minutes. It'll be sticky. Divide in half. Powder with dry flour to shape and place into 2 greased pans. Cover with towel and let rise 1 hour. Bake 375 degrees for about 1 hour. It will sound hollow on bottom. Remove from pan and butter tops right away.

Orange-Walnut Bread

2 large oranges
1 cup water
1 cup sugar (granulated)
$^1/_2$ cup packed brown sugar
2 tablespoons butter or margarine
3 cups sifted flour
1 teaspoon salt
3 teaspoons baking powder
1 egg
1 cup milk
$^1/_2$ cup chopped walnuts

Pare rind very thin from oranges, then slice into thin strips. (Rind should be paper thin - no white.) Simmer in water in saucepan 30 minutes, then drain. Combine granulated and brown sugars and butter with orange rind in same saucepan. Heat, stirring constantly, 5 minutes or 'til butter melts and sugars dissolve. Set aside. Sift flour, baking powder, and salt in medium sized bowl. Beat egg in small bowl, stir in milk, then orange-rind/sugar mixture. Stir into dry ingredients, just until blended; stir in walnuts. Pour into greased 9 x 5 x 3 inch pan. Bake 350 degrees for 1 hour. Cool in pan 5 minutes. Turn out cool. Store 1 day before slicing.

Make a loaf each of Date Tea Bread and Orange-Walnut Bread. Cut thin slices of each bread and spread one slice with cream cheese. Sandwich together with a slice of the other bread. Cut into triangles to serve.

Feather Rolls

2 packages dry yeast
$^1/_4$ cup sugar
$^1/_2$ cup shortening
1 teaspoon salt
5 cups flour
2-$^1/_2$ cups evaporated milk

Dissolve yeast in $^1/_4$ cup milk at lukewarm temperature. Scald remaining milk and pour over salt, sugar, and shortening. When dissolved, cool to luke-warm and stir in yeast mixture. Add flour. Beat well. Let rise in warm place (set bowl over very warm water; this helps it rise quickly). Fill muffin tins $^2/_3$ full. Let rise. Bake in 375 degree oven 'til brown.

Never Fail Pie Crust

1-$^1/_2$ cups shortening
4 cups flour
$^1/_2$ cup cold water
1 tablespoon vinegar
1 tablespoon sugar
$^1/_2$ tablespoon salt
1 egg

Mix flour, sugar, and salt with shortening. Add egg, water, and vinegar gradu-ally to other ingredients. Mix flour until moistened well. Roll out on floured board. Makes four pie crusts. Bake in 425 degree oven for 12 to 15 minutes.

Carrot Walnut Bread

1-$^1/_2$ cups finely grated raw carrots
1 cup firmly packed brown sugar
1 teaspoon grated fresh orange peel
1 tablespoon vegetable oil
1 cup boiling water
2 eggs, beaten
1-$^1/_2$ cups unsifted all-purpose flour
1 cup unsifted whole wheat flour
2-$^1/_2$ teaspoons baking powder
1 teaspoon baking soda
1 teaspoon salt
1 cup chopped walnuts

Combine carrots, brown sugar, grated orange peel, vegetable oil, and water in large bowl. Mix well. Set aside to cool. Stir eggs into carrot mixture. Mix and sift flour, baking powder, baking soda, and salt. Blend into carrot mixture. Stir in walnuts. Turn into well greased 9 x 5 x 3 inch loaf pan. Let stand 5 minutes. Bake at 350 degrees 50–60 minutes until cake tester, inserted in center of bread, comes out clean. Remove from pan. Cool on wire rack. Wrap in foil or plastic wrap. Let stand overnight at room temperature before slicing.

My beautiful sister, Willadeene, dressed to model new fashions at my sister Rachel's boutique, "9 to 5."

CASSEROLES

Company Tuna Bake

1 3-ounce package cream cheese
1 6-$^1/_2$– or 9-$^1/_2$– ounce can
   tuna (drained)
1 tablespoon onion
1 tablespoon prepared mustard
1 cup small salad macaroni

1 can mushroom soup
1-$^1/_2$ tablespoons pimento
   (chopped)
$^1/_4$ cup milk
$^1/_2$ cup bread crumbs

Place macaroni in a large pot and cook according to directions. Drain. In a large bowl, mix all ingredients except bread crumbs. Place in casserole dish. Sprinkle with crumb topping and bake at 300 degrees about 30 minutes.

Garlic Noodles

1 8-ounce package egg noodles
1 small package sour cream
1 small onion (finely chopped)
Tabasco Sauce
$^1/_2$ teaspoon garlic
bread crumbs

1 3-ounce package cream cheese
   (softened)
$^1/_2$ stick butter or margarine
Worcestershire Sauce
dash pepper

In large pot, cook noodles per directions. Drain. While noodles are hot, mix the remaining ingredients except crumbs. Pour into a buttered casserole dish and top with bread crumbs. Cover with foil until the last few minutes. Bake at 350 degrees for 30 minutes.

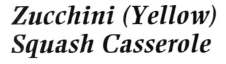

Zucchini (Yellow) Squash Casserole

6 large zucchinis
1 egg
1 green onion (optional)
butter or margarine
cracker crumbs
1 cup sour cream
$^1/_2$ cup or more grated Cheddar cheese
salt

In large pot, cut zucchini into $^1/_2$ inch slices; simmer in $^1/_4$ cup of water until almost done. Drain. In a separate pan, add sour cream, Cheddar cheese, butter, and a little salt. Heat slowly until cheese melts. Add one beaten egg. In a buttered casserole dish, pour cheese mixture over the zucchini. Top with buttered cracker crumbs and grated cheese. Bake about 25 minutes at 350 degrees until heated through.

Mom looking a bit Hollywood on a family trip on Dolly's bus.

Zucchini Casserole

1 large onion (approximately 1 cup diced)
1 egg
1-$^1/_2$ cups minute rice (cooked)
1 teaspoon basil
1 large zucchini
salt and pepper
1-$^1/_2$ pounds ground beef
1 cup cottage cheese
1 can tomato sauce
1-$^1/_2$ teaspoons oregano
mozzarella cheese

Sauté onion in large skillet. Add ground beef and simmer until beef crumbles. Drain off excess liquid. Stir in egg, rice, tomato sauce, basil, oregano, salt, and pepper to taste.

Parboil the zucchini. Drain. If you do not have fresh, use canned in tomato sauce. In a casserole dish, spread a layer of meat mixture. Put zucchini on top and sprinkle with mozzarella cheese. Repeat layers with remaining mixture. Bake at 350 degrees covered about 10 minutes or until cheese crusts and browns. Makes 8 to 10 large servings.

Can substitute soy burger for beef. Use 1-$^1/_2$ cups burger mix.

Broccoli & Rice Casserole

1 10-ounce package frozen chopped broccoli
$^1/_2$ cup onion sautéed in butter
1 cup cooked rice
1 can cream of mushroom soup
$^1/_2$ cup diced celery

Combine all ingredients in a casserole dish. Bake at 325 degrees for 45 minutes. (To double recipe, use another can of cream of mushroom soup or cream of celery soup.) Serves 4.

Sautéed Chicken Cutlets

2 whole chicken breasts
$^1/_2$ cup grated parmesan cheese
2 tablespoons butter
$^1/_2$ teaspoon thyme
$^1/_2$ cup bread crumbs
2 eggs, beaten
$^1/_2$ teaspoon basil

Skin and bone chicken breasts. Dip chicken in beaten egg. Coat on each side in bread crumbs mixed with cheese and herbs. In hot skillet with oil, sauté for 4 minutes on each side.

Frito Casserole

I first made this in home economics class in high school. I love it. My home ec. teacher, Mrs. Ogle, was certainly an influence on my desire to become a serious cook.

1 medium package Fritos
1 large can chili
1 package grated Cheddar cheese
1 medium onion (chopped)
1 package grated mozzarella cheese

Crush a layer of Fritos in the bottom of a greased pan. Layer with chili, onions, and cheese. Repeat layers with remaining mixture. Bake at 350 degrees for one half hour. Serves 6.

Porter Wagoner and me at a Fan Fair interview sharing a laugh.

Zucchini Mexicoli

$^1/_4$ cup cooking oil
1 large carrot (shredded 1 cup)
1 large onion (chopped 1 cup)
dash pepper
$^1/_4$ teaspoon basil
2 teaspoons prepared mustard
salt
1 pound zucchini (peeled and thinly
      sliced 2 to 4 cups)
$^1/_2$ medium green pepper (thin strips)
$^1/_2$ teaspoon garlic salt
$^1/_3$ cup taco sauce
2 medium tomatoes (cut into wedges)

Serves a bunch and it's really good.

Heat oil in 10 inch skillet. Add vegetables, garlic, salt, basil, and pepper. Toss to mix well. Cook covered over medium high heat for 4 minutes. Stir. Toss occasionally. Combine taco sauce and mustard in small bowl. Stir into vegetables. Add tomato wedges and cook uncovered 3 to 5 minutes or until heated through. Season with salt and serve. Use Old El Paso Enchilada Sauce (Hot) for the taco sauce. Serve with grated sharp Cheddar cheese or mozzarella cheese on each serving.

Broccoli Casserole

1 box frozen broccoli
$^1/_2$ cup mayonnaise
1 grated onion (small)
$^1/_2$ cup grated cheese

$^1/_2$ can mushroom soup
Cheez-it crackers
1 egg, beaten
salt and pepper

In a medium pan, cook broccoli according to package directions. Cool and chop. Combine remaining ingredients (except crackers) and add to broccoli. Put in buttered casserole dish and sprinkle Cheez-it crackers on top. Bake at 350 degrees for 20 minutes. Serves 6 to 8.

Texas Hash

2 onions (sliced)
3 tablespoons cooking oil
$^1/_2$ cup canned tomatoes
1 teaspoon salt
$^1/_2$ cup uncooked rice

2 green peppers
1 pound ground beef
1 teaspoon chili powder
$^1/_4$ teaspoon pepper

In a large skillet, cook onions and peppers in oil until onions are yellow. Add beef and stir until mixture falls apart. Add tomatoes, rice, and seasonings. Put mixture in a large casserole. Cover and bake in moderately hot oven, about 375 degrees, for 45 minutes or until done.

Great recipe. You can substitute soy burger for beef if you like.

Chicken Dressing

12 slices day old bread
2 cups chicken broth
1 cup chicken, cooked and boned
$^1/_4$ cup onion, diced and cooked
1 can cream of mushroom soup
3 eggs
1 teaspoon rubbed sage

In large mixing bowl, break bread into bite-size portions. Stir in remaining ingredients. Mix well. Put into a well-greased casserole dish, cover and bake for 50 minutes at 300 degrees.

Tuna Noodle Casserole

1 6-$^1/_2$-ounce can tuna
2 cups cooked noodles
$^1/_4$ cup mayonnaise
$^1/_2$ cup celery (chopped)
2 tablespoons green pepper (chopped)
$^1/_4$ teaspoon salt

1 can cream of mushroom soup
$^1/_3$ cup Colby or Cheddar cheese (grated)
$^1/_4$ cup onion (chopped)
2 tablespoons pimento (chopped)
1 tablespoon lemon juice

In a large mixing bowl, combine all ingredients. Put in a large casserole dish and bake for 30 to 35 minutes at 350 degrees.

Tuna Burgers

1 7-ounce can tuna
1 small onion (chopped)
6 hamburger buns
$^1/_4$ cup mayonnaise
1 cup chopped celery
$^1/_2$ cup diced American cheese
$^1/_2$ cup chopped ripe olives
salt and pepper

Split and butter hamburger buns. In a mixing bowl, combine all other ingredients. Fill buns with tuna mixture. Place in paper bags or aluminum foil. Heat in 350 degrees oven 15 to 20 minutes.

Dumplings like Grandma Messer Made

2 cups flour
2 teaspoons baking powder
$^1/_2$ teaspoon salt
$^1/_2$–$^3/_4$ cup hot water
3 tablespoons shortening

In a mixing bowl, work the shortening into the dry ingredients with a pastry blender. Add the hot water and mix to form a soft dough. Roll out on a floured board. Cut into squares. Drop into boiling broth. Cook until tender.

Canadian Pork Pie

1-$^1/_2$ pounds lean boneless pork
$^1/_2$ cup chopped onion
1 clove garlic (minced)
1 cup beef bouillon
$^1/_2$ teaspoon chervil (optional)
$^1/_4$ teaspoon mace
top and bottom pie crust
2 slices bacon (diced)
$^1/_2$ cup chopped celery
2 tablespoons flour
1 small bay leaf
1 tablespoon butter or margarine (melted)
1 teaspoon salt

In large skillet, lightly brown bacon. Add pork, onion, celery, and garlic. Cook, stirring frequently until meat is brown. Sprinkle flour over top. Add bouillon, salt, and spices, and mix. Cook slowly until mixture thickens. Cover and cook slowly 30 minutes. Cool 10 minutes.

Fill crust lined pan with pork mixture. Moisten crust rim. Cover with top crust. Fold edges under and flute. Brush melted butter over top. Bake 425 degrees for 15 minutes. Reduce heat to 350 degrees and bake for 25 minutes.

Spaghetti Crust Pie

$^1/_2$ pound cooked hamburger *
6 ounces spaghetti, cooked
2 eggs
8 ounces pizza sauce
1-$^1/_2$ cups mozzarella cheese (grated)
2 tablespoons butter
$^1/_3$ cup grated Parmesan cheese
1 medium onion (cooked in 2 table-
    spoons butter)

Grease a 9 inch pie pan. In a large mixing bowl, mix eggs, hamburger, and onion together. Put cooked spaghetti in bottom of greased pie pan. Spread mixture over spaghetti. Top with pizza sauce, then mozzarella cheese and Parmesan. Bake for 20 minutes at 350 degrees.

* I substitute 1 cup soyburger for hamburger. It tastes just as good!

Daddy, Dolly, and Mom at a Fan Fair celebration some years ago.

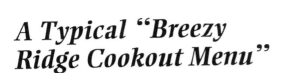

A Typical "Breezy Ridge Cookout Menu"

5 pounds great northern beans
12 pounds hickory smoked ham
15 pounds potatoes (2 iron skillets of
    fried potatoes)
4 pounds turnips (1 iron skillet of
    turnips)
5 pounds sauerkraut cooked with 3
    pounds Polish sausage
6 pounds coleslaw
iced tea and coffee
blackberry cobbler
dump cakes
several pans of piping hot cornbread
lots of fun and laughter

A typo in the original recipe indicated 51 pounds of beans instead of five. I guess we could have named this "A Typical Breezy Ridge Blow Out."

DESSERTS

Dump Cake

1 package yellow cake mix
1 15-ounce can cherry pie filling
1 cup chopped pecans
1 15-ounce can crushed pineapple in syrup
$^{1}/_{2}$ cup margarine (1 stick)

Dump pineapple in pan, spread. Dump in cherry pie filling. Dump cake mix in, spread. Slice margarine over and sprinkle pecans. Bake at 350 degrees 48 to 53 minutes. So good and rich.

Dan's Impossible Pie

$^{1}/_{2}$ cup Bisquick
1 cup sugar
4 eggs
$^{1}/_{2}$ teaspoon salt
$^{1}/_{2}$ stick butter

2 cups milk
1 teaspoon vanilla
$^{1}/_{2}$ cup raisins ($^{1}/_{2}$ cup coconut
    can be substituted)
nutmeg

Mix all ingredients except raisins (coconut) in blender. Blend until well mixed. Pour into ungreased deep pie pan. Sprinkle raisins over mixture so they are evenly distributed. Sprinkle top with freshly ground nutmeg. Bake for 55 minutes at 350 degree oven.

Desserts

Angie's Simple Cake

3 cups flour
2 teaspoons soda
1 teaspoon salt
2 cups sugar
4 tablespoons cocoa
12 tablespoons vegetable oil
2 tablespoons vinegar
2 teaspoons vanilla
2 cups water

Sift dry ingredients together and put in a 9 x 12 inch baking pan. Make 3 holes in the dry ingredients. Pour 12 tablespoons vegetable oil in one hole, 2 tablespoons vinegar in the second hole, and 2 teaspoons vanilla in the third hole. Pour 2 cups water over everything in the pan. Mix together with a fork stirring well. Bake at 350 degrees 25 to 30 minutes. Cool. Frost.

Icing

$^1/_4$ cup butter
1 cup sugar
3 tablespoons cocoa
$^1/_3$ cup milk

Stir all ingredients together in a saucepan until mixture boils. Boil one minute. Set pan in cold water and beat until thickened. Spread over cake.

This moist, chocolate cake is a family favorite. It is especially good if someone has an allergy to milk or eggs since neither is an ingredient. This recipe can be cut in half for one square cake.

Bessie's Canadian Butter Tarts

**pastry for 24 tart shells
(any pie crust recipe)**
$1/_2$ cup raisins plumped in boiling water
$1/_2$ cup firmly packed brown sugar
1 cup corn syrup
dash of salt
$1/_4$ cup soft butter
2 egg yolks
1 teaspoon vanilla
2 egg whites

Line tart pans with pastry. Sprinkle raisins in bottom of each. In large bowl, cream butter and sugar. Beat in egg yolks, corn syrup, vanilla, and salt. Beat whites until stiff and fold in. Spoon into tart shell, filling $3/_4$ full. Bake at 375 degrees for 15 minutes. Bake on rack placed below center of oven so pastry will bake before filling browns too much. Bake until brown for a smooth surface (don't allow to bubble). If it does, reduce heat a little. Cool in pan.

Blueberry
Cheese Cake

2 cups graham cracker crumbs
$^1/_4$ cup melted butter
1 teaspoon vanilla
1 can blueberry pie filling (or
    thickened fresh blueberries)

1-$^1/_2$ cups sugar
2 eggs
1 pound cream cheese

Make crust by mixing graham cracker crumbs with $^1/_2$ cup sugar and the melted butter. Pat in a 9 x 12 inch pan. In a bowl, blend eggs, 1 cup sugar, cream cheese, and vanilla. Spread this mixture over crumbs in pan. Bake at 375 degrees for 15 minutes. When cool, spread the blueberry filling over it. Chill overnight in refrigerator before serving. Cool Whip or whipped cream can be used as a topping.

Old Time
Matrimony Cake

1 cup brown sugar
1-$^1/_2$ cups flour
$^3/_4$ teaspoon baking soda
1 pound dates

2 cups rolled oats
1 teaspoon baking powder
$^3/_4$ cup butter
1 teaspoon vanilla

Mix ingredients, except dates and vanilla, like a pie crust. Cook dates (simmer chopped dates in $^1/_2$ cup of butter and $^1/_3$ cup of brown sugar, both amounts are in addition to quantities listed in ingredients, for 5 minutes). When cool, add vanilla. Put $^1/_2$ of the crumbs in a 9 x 13 inch pan and pat down hard. Spread on the date mixture then the rest of the crumbs on top. Pat down again. Bake for 30 minutes in a 325 to 350 degree oven.

Pat's Flan

12 egg yolks
1 can condensed sweetened milk
1 teaspoon vanilla
1 cup sugar
1 can evaporated milk

Beat egg yolks and sugar. Add condensed milk, evaporated milk, and vanilla. Caramelize 2 teaspoons sugar in 8 inch pan. Add mixture. Steam or bake in water under pan at 350 degrees for one hour.

Meringue

2 cups egg whites
2 tablespoons vanilla
2 tablespoons vinegar
4 cups sugar

Beat egg whites. Add vinegar and vanilla while beating. Add sugar. Bake at 250 degrees for 3 hours on foil lined pan.

Violet Bell's Old Fashioned Jam Cake

1 cup shortening (butter)
1 cup raisins (chopped)
4 eggs
4 cups flour
1 teaspoon baking soda (add to milk)
1 teaspoon cinnamon
1 teaspoon nutmeg
$^1/_2$ cup nuts
2 cups brown sugar
2 cups jam (blackberry jam with seeds)
1 cup sour milk or buttermilk
1 teaspoon baking powder
1 teaspoon allspice
1 teaspoon vanilla

In large mixing bowl, mix above ingredients together. Pour into 3 greased and floured cake pans. Bake 350 degrees for 35 to 40 minutes. Mom cuts a circle of waxed paper to fit the pan bottom and greases and flours it.

Icing

2 cups brown sugar
1 cup cream
$^1/_2$ stick butter
$^1/_2$ box raisins (chopped)
1 pound nuts (chopped)

Mix all ingredients in saucepan and cook this icing until thickened and suitable to spread. Ice between layers, top, and sides of cake.

Sallie Messer's Cocoa Pie

1-$^1/_2$ cups milk
$^1/_3$ cup cocoa
1 teaspoon butter
pinch of salt

2 eggs, separated
1 cup sugar
2 tablespoons flour
2 teaspoons vanilla

In saucepan, heat 1 cup of milk and butter. In mixing bowl, dissolve sugar, cocoa, and salt with remaining milk. Add well-beaten egg yolks and vanilla. Gradually add flour, stirring constantly to prevent lumps. Slowly pour mixture into hot milk and butter. Cook until thickened. Pour into baked pie shell. Beat egg white until stiff. Put meringue on pie and bake at 400 degrees until brown.

Grandma Messer's Lemon Pie

3 egg yolks
2 tablespoons flour
1 pint hot water
1 cup sugar (heaping)
2 lemons, juice only
1 tablespoon butter

Cook all ingredients until thick in a double boiler. Pour into cooked pie shell. Beat egg whites to make a meringue. Bake to brown meringue 12 to 15 minutes at 350 degrees. Pie crust recipe on page 37.

Grandma Messer's Devil's Food Cake

2 cups sugar
4 eggs
1 teaspoon baking soda
2 cups flour
1 teaspoon vanilla
$^3/_4$ cup butter
$^3/_4$ cup cocoa
$^1/_2$ cup boiling water
1 cup sour milk

In large mixing bowl, pour hot water over cocoa and soda and cool. Cream sugar and butter. Add eggs, vanilla, cocoa, then milk and flour alternately. Bake at 350 degrees for 40 minutes.

A pizza party at my place with Cassie, Rachel, Rebecca, and Hannah. We call these get-togethers sister fixes.

Mississippi Mud Cake

2 cups sugar
4 eggs
1 cup chopped nuts
1 cup butter
1-$^1/_2$ cups flour
1 teaspoon vanilla
1 teaspoon baking powder
3 squares unsweetened chocolate

Melt chocolate and butter on very low heat. Beat eggs til foamy, then add sugar. Mix in all other ingredients. Pour into a greased 13 x 9 inch pan. Bake at 350 degrees for 30 minutes. While cake is hot, melt marshmallow on the top. Let cake cool.

Icing

3 squares unsweetened chocolate
1 small can evaporated milk
1 cup sugar (granulated)
1 teaspoon vanilla
$^1/_2$ cup margarine
1 box confectioners' sugar

Melt chocolate, margarine, milk, and sugar 'til well blended on low heat. Mix in confectioner's sugar and vanilla. Spread on top of cooled cake.

This recipe is by Carolyn Cross. She is like a sister to me and one of the best cooks in the South.

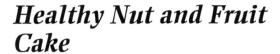

Healthy Nut and Fruit Cake

1 cup safflower oil
3 cups rolled oats
1-$^1/_2$ cups shredded, unsweetened
    coconut
2 large oranges
1 teaspoon vanilla
$^1/_2$ cup frozen apple juice (concentrated,
    no water added)
1 cup chopped pecans
1 cup drained, crushed pineapple
1-$^1/_2$ cups fresh cranberries (or 2 pack-
    ages frozen relish)
2 large apples
2-$^1/_2$ cups whole wheat flour

Coarsely grind cranberries, oranges, and
apples. Combine all ingredients stirring until
well moistened. If too dry, add more apple
juice. If too thin to resemble cake batter, add
more rolled oats. Spoon into a lightly greased
bundt pan and bake at 350 degrees for 50 to
60 minutes or until done. Let cool in pan for
10 minutes before turning out. Good when
eaten as a cake, but also good when sliced and
toasted in toaster oven.

Sallie Messer's Baked Date Pudding

1 egg
2 cups flour
1 cup nuts
enough milk to make a stiff batter
1 cup sugar
1 pound dates
5 teaspoons baking powder

Combine in large mixing bowl sugar, flour, and baking powder. Add fruit, nuts, egg, and milk to make batter for cake.

Sauce

2 cups brown sugar
3 tablespoons butter
2 cups water

Boil sauce for 5 minutes in saucepan. Pour sauce in bottom of baking dish and pour batter over. Bake in moderate oven 350 degrees until sauce bubbles up to top and cake is done.

*Modeling my Western/Latin
ensemble in Holland, backstage
at a summer festival.*

Rainbow Cake

2 baked 8-inch or 9-inch white layer cakes (cooled)
2 cups boiling water
2 packages (3 ounces each) Jell-O (any flavors)
1 8-ounce container of Cool Whip, thawed

Place cake layers, top sides up, in two clean layer pans. Prick each cake with utility fork at $^1/_2$-inch intervals. Dissolve each flavor Jell-O separately in 1 cup of the boiling water and carefully spoon each over one of the cake layers. Chill 3 to 4 hours. Dip one cake pan in warm water for 10 seconds; turn out onto serving plate. Top with 1 cup of the whipped topping. Unmold second layer cake. Place carefully on first layers. Frost top and sides with remaining whipped topping. Chill. Garnish as desired.

Showing off my new perfume, "Chapeau," at the Hat House.

Butter Pecan Turtle Bar Cookies

Crust

2 cups flour
$^1/_2$ cup butter
1 cup brown sugar

Filling

1 cup pecan halves
$^1/_2$ cup brown sugar
$^2/_3$ cup butter

Topping

1 cup chocolate chips

Combine crust ingredients in 3 quart mixing bowl. Mix at high speed 2 to 3 minutes or until mixture is very fine. Pat firmly into ungreased 13 x 9 x 2 inch pan. Sprinkle 1 cup pecan halves evenly over unbaked crust.

Make caramel layer of $^2/_3$ cup butter and $^1/_2$ cup brown sugar. Cook over medium heat stirring constantly until mixture begins to boil. Boil $^1/_2$ to 1 minute. Pour evenly over pecans and crust. Bake at 350 degrees for 18 to 22 minutes or until caramel layer is bubbly and crust is light brown. Remove from oven. Immediately sprinkle 1 cup chocolate chips on top. Allow chips to melt 2 to 3 minutes, then slightly swirl chips with knife as they melt. Do not spread though. Cool completely before cutting into bars.

Chess Pie

Preheat oven to 350 degrees.

$^1/_2$ cup melted butter
1 cup sugar (or $^3/_4$ cup raw honey)
2 whole eggs
1 tablespoon cornmeal
1 teaspoon vinegar
1 teaspoon vanilla
unbaked pie shell

Mix all ingredients in large bowl. Pour mixture into unbaked pie shell and bake at 350 degrees for 35 to 40 minutes. Serve when cool.

French Chocolate Pie

$^1/_2$ cup butter
2 squares unsweetened chocolate
2 cups thawed Cool Whip
$^3/_4$ cup sugar
2 eggs
baked pie shell

Cream butter with sugar in large bowl. Stir in cooled melted chocolate. Add eggs, one at a time, beating well after each addition on high speed for 4 to 5 minutes. Fold in Cool Whip. Pour into a cooled baked pie shell. Chill until firm, about 2 hours, or freeze.

Coffee Pecan Pie

3 eggs, beaten
$^3/_4$ cup white corn syrup
2 tablespoons melted butter
1 teaspoon vanilla
1 cup pecans, chopped

$^3/_4$ cup molasses
$^1/_2$ cup strong coffee
$^1/_4$ teaspoon salt
4 tablespoons flour

Preheat oven to 400 degrees for 15 minutes. In large mixing bowl, combine pecans and flour. Stir in remaining ingredients and mix well. Pour into pie shell and bake at 400 degrees for 20 minutes to start and 325 degrees for 30 minutes until done.

Frozen Lemonade Fluff Pie

1 tablespoon gelatin
4 egg yolks (beaten)
1 6-ounce can frozen lemonade
cup cream

$^1/_2$ cup cold water
dash salt
4 egg whites
baked pie shell

In top of double boiler soften gelatin in $^1/_2$ cup water. Add egg yolks and salt, and cook until gelatin dissolves and mixture is slightly thick (about 5 minutes). Remove from heat. Stir in lemonade (concentrated). Chill until mixture mounds when spooned. Beat egg whites to soft peaks. Fold into gelatin mixture. Whip 1 cup cream, fold $^1/_2$ into gelatin mixture. Put all in baked pastry shell. Serve rest of whipped cream on top of pie when it is cool.

Pineapple
Sour Cream Pie

$^3/_4$ cup sugar
1 cup crushed pineapple
2 tablespoons lemon juice
$^1/_8$ teaspoon salt
$^1/_4$ cup flour

1 cup sour cream
2 egg yolks
$^1/_4$ cup sugar (add to meringue)
$^1/_8$ teaspoon cream of tartar
2 egg whites

Combine $^3/_4$ cup sugar and the flour in the top of double boiler. Add pineapple, sour cream, lemon juice, and salt. Cook over direct heat stirring constantly until mixture thickens. Then place over boiling water. Beat egg yolks slightly. Stir in little of hot mixture and pour back into double boiler. Cook and stir for just 2 minutes longer. Remove from heat and cool. Beat egg whites with cream of tartar and $^1/_4$ cup sugar until soft peaks stand. Put on pie and brown.

Apricot Dessert

1 small angel food cake
1 package orange Jell-O
1 15-ounce can apricots
1 pint cream, whipped

Drain fruit. Add water to juice to make 2 cups. In a saucepan, bring juice to a boil and pour over Jell-O. Let cool. Add fruit, chopped up a little or mashed. Let set until it starts to congeal. Fold in whipped cream and gently mix with broken pieces of angel food cake. Put in pan and refrigerate.

Graham Cracker Pie

Hint: Always heat milk for soft pies and you won't have to stir over the fire as long.

16 graham crackers (rolled fine)
$^1/_2$ cup melted butter
$^1/_4$ cup sugar

In large bowl, mix ingredients together and line large pie pan, reserving $^1/_2$ cup for topping.

Filling

1 cup milk
3 tablespoons flour
$^3/_4$ cup sugar
3 egg yolks
1 cup half and half
1 tablespoon cornstarch
$^1/_4$ teaspoon salt
1 teaspoon vanilla

Mix all ingredients except egg yolks and vanilla in large sauce pan or double boiler. Cook over medium heat until it thickens. Add egg yolks (beaten). Cook 2 or 3 minutes more. Add vanilla. Pour into graham cracker crust. Make meringue of the egg whites left from yolks. Spread on top of filling. Sprinkle reserved crumbs on top and bake until brown in 375 degree oven, 10 to 15 minutes.

No Bake Peanut Butter Pie

1 8-ounce package cream cheese
$^1/_3$ cup peanut butter (smooth)
1-$^1/_2$ pints whipping cream
1 cup sugar
3 eggs
1 teaspoon vanilla

In large bowl, cream until real smooth cream cheese, sugar, and peanut butter. Set aside. Wash beaters, dry. Separate the eggs. Add 1 yolk at a time and beat smooth. Wash beaters again. Dry. Whip the cream. Beat the egg whites. Fold in egg whites, vanilla, and whipped cream and put in graham cracker crust. Freeze.

Coconut Custard Pie

4 eggs
$^1/_4$ teaspoon salt
2-$^1/_2$ cups milk (scalded)
1 9-inch unbaked pie shell
   (chilled)

2 tablespoons soft butter
2 cups granulated sugar
1 teaspoon vanilla
3-$^1/_2$ ounces coconut
$^1/_4$ cup brown sugar

In large bowl, beat eggs. Slightly stir in granulated sugar, salt, and vanilla. Gradually stir in milk and coconut, reserving $^1/_2$ cup coconut for top. Pour into pastry shell. Bake in hot oven (400 degrees) 25 to 30 minutes or until knife inserted half way between outside and center of pie comes out clean. Cool. Just before serving, mix reserved coconut, brown sugar and butter. Sprinkle on top of pie. Broil 3 to 4 minutes until lightly brown.

Stella Parton's Country Cookin'

Rhubarb Cream Pie

1-$^1/_2$ cups sugar
3 teaspoons nutmeg
4 cups rhubarb (sliced)
$^1/_4$ cup flour
3 lightly beaten eggs
2 tablespoons butter or margarine

In large mixing bowl, blend flour, sugar, and nutmeg. Add to eggs. Beat until smooth. Add rhubarb. Pour into 9 inch pastry lined pie pan. Dot with butter. Top with lattice crust. Bake at 400 degrees 50 to 60 minutes. Cool.

Japanese Fruit Pie

2 sticks margarine
2 cups sugar
1 cup chopped pecans
4 eggs, slightly beaten
1 cup raisins
2 tablespoons vinegar

Melt margarine. Cool. Add rest of ingredients. Put into two unbaked pie shells. Bake at 325 degrees for 40 minutes. Best served warm. Freezes well.

Sin Pie

Crust

1 cup flour
1 cup chopped pecans
1 stick butter, melted

Mix ingredients well and spread in 9 x 13 inch pan. Bake at 350 degrees 20 minutes. Let cool completely.

1st Layer

1 cup confectioners sugar
1 cup Cool Whip
1 8-ounce package cream cheese

Beat all ingredients and spread on crust.

2nd Layer

1 package chocolate instant pudding
2-$^1/_8$ cups milk
3 tablespoons cocoa
1 package vanilla instant pudding

Beat ingredients until smooth. Spread on top. Top with Cool Whip and refrigerate.

Scandinavian concert tour '93. I always have a great time with the audiences in Europe and Scandinavia.

Stella Parton's Country Cookin'

Ugly Duckling Pudding Cake

1 package 2 layer cake (yellow) mix
1 16-ounce can fruit cocktail,
        including syrup
4 eggs
$^1/_2$ cup brown sugar
1 package instant pudding
1 cup flake coconut
$^1/_4$ cup oil
$^1/_2$ cup chopped nuts

Mix all ingredients in large mixing bowl. Bake
in 9 x 13 inch pan, greased and floured. Bake
in 325 degree oven 45 minutes or until done.
Do not under-bake.

Hot Butter Glaze

$^1/_2$ cup sugar
$^1/_2$ cup evaporated milk
$^1/_2$ stick butter
1-$^1/_2$ cups flake coconut

In a saucepan, boil sugar, milk, and butter for 2
minutes. Stir in flake coconut. Spread glaze
over cooled cake.

German Sweet Chocolate Cake

1 4-ounce bar German Sweet
   Chocolate
2 cups sugar
1 teaspoon vanilla
$^1/_2$ teaspoon salt
1 teaspoon baking soda
4 egg whites, stiffly beaten
$^1/_2$ cup boiling water
1 cup margarine or butter
4 egg yolks, unbeaten

2-$^1/_2$ cups sifted cake flour
1 cup buttermilk
Coconut Pecan Frosting
1 cup evaporated milk
3 egg yolks
1 teaspoon vanilla
1 cup chopped pecans
1 cup sugar
$^1/_2$ cup butter or margarine
1-$^1/_2$ cups flake coconut

Melt chocolate in boiling water in bowl. Cool. In larger mixing bowl, cream butter and sugar until fluffy. Add egg yolks one at a time and beat well after each. Add melted chocolate and vanilla and mix well. Sift together flour, salt, and soda. Add alternately with buttermilk to chocolate mixture. Beat well until smooth. Fold in egg whites. Pour into three deep 8 or 9 inch layer pans lined on bottom with wax paper. Bake in 350 degree oven 30 to 40 minutes. Cool. Frost tops only.

Coconut Pecan Frosting

1 cup evaporated milk
3 egg yolks
1 teaspoon vanilla
1 cup chopped pecans

1 cup sugar
$^1/_2$ cup butter or margarine
1-$^1/_2$ cups flake coconut

In saucepan, combine evaporated milk, sugar, egg yolks, butter, and vanilla. Cook over medium heat until thickened, about 12 minutes. Add flake coconut and pecans. Beat until thick enough to spread. Makes 2-$^1/_2$ cups.

Stella Parton's Country Cookin'

Miss Margrette's Chess Pie

3 whole eggs
1 teaspoon vinegar
1 tablespoon vanilla
1-$^1/_2$ cups sugar
$^1/_4$ pound butter or margarine

Melt butter or margarine. In large bowl, add butter to rest of ingredients. Stir well. Pour into pie shell and bake at 350 degrees for 15 minutes, then 325 degrees about 20 minutes. Butter is best in this, but who wants to die of cholesterol? Oh, well. It's to die for.

Peanut Butter Fudge

$^1/_2$ cup butter or margarine
$^1/_2$ cup milk
$^3/_4$ cup smooth or crunchy peanut butter
1 pound light golden brown sugar
1 teaspoon vanilla
1 pound confectioners sugar

In a medium saucepan, melt butter and stir in brown sugar and milk. Bring to a boil and stir 2 minutes. Remove from heat. Stir in peanut butter and vanilla. Mix in confectioners sugar. Beat until smooth. Spread into buttered 9 inch square baking pan. Chill until firm. Cut into squares. Makes 3-$^1/_2$ pounds.

Lemon Velvet Cake

1 package lemon cake mix
4 whole eggs
$^3/_4$ cup oil
1 package lemon instant pudding
$^3/_4$ cup water

Grease and flour large Pyrex pan. Set oven to 350 degrees. In large mixing bowl, mix ingredients. Bake for 35 minutes.

Topping

$^1/_3$ cup orange juice
2 cups powdered sugar
2 tablespoons salad oil

Mix all ingredients together. While cake is still hot, punch holes all over top with fork and pour on topping.

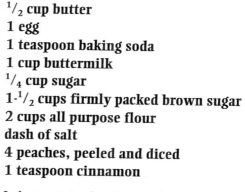

Fresh Peach Cake

$^1/_2$ cup butter
1 egg
1 teaspoon baking soda
1 cup buttermilk
$^1/_4$ cup sugar
1-$^1/_2$ cups firmly packed brown sugar
2 cups all purpose flour
dash of salt
4 peaches, peeled and diced
1 teaspoon cinnamon

In large mixing bowl, cream butter and brown sugar until light and fluffy. Beat in egg. Sift flour with soda and salt. Add to creamed mixture. Alternate with buttermilk, beating until smooth after each addition. Gently blend in peaches. Pour batter into greased 13 x 9 inch pan. Sprinkle sugar and cinnamon over top and bake at 350 degrees 30 to 35 minutes or until cake loosens from sides and tests done.

Riding in the spring parade in Pigeon Forge, Tennessee, in May '94

Pistachio Cake

1 package white cake mix
4 large eggs
$^1/_2$ cup chopped nuts
$^1/_2$ cup water
$^1/_2$ cup milk
2 packages pistachio instant pudding
(reserve 2 or 3 teaspoons)
$^1/_2$ cup vegetable oil

Mix cake mix and pudding mix. Save 2 to 3 teaspoons of the pudding for frosting. Add milk, oil, water, and eggs. Mix at low speed 2 minutes, then 3 minutes at high speed. Fold in nuts. Pour into greased 13 x 9 x 2 inch cake pan. Bake 50 to 60 minutes at 350 degrees. When cool, frost with following: Small amount of Cool Whip mixed with balance of pudding (2 to 3 teaspoons.)

My sister, Cassie, and her husband, Larry, at another family feast.

Vinegar Taffy

2 cups sugar
2 tablespoons butter
a few grains of salt
$^1/_8$ teaspoon cream of tartar
$^1/_2$ cup vinegar

Cook all ingredients in a pan on medium heat until it reaches the hard crack stage on a candy thermometer or until it makes a string that will harden and crack when dropped in cold water. After taffy has reached this stage, pour into a buttered pan to cool some. Now comes the fun part. Butter hand generously. Caution...Taffy holds the heat and is sticky and will cling to the skin and burn so don't let small children pull until it cools or you have pulled it first. Take a spoon of the taffy from the pan when it is cool enough to handle. (Taffy will be honey colored.) Keeping hands well buttered, start pulling taffy out into a string and roping it back together. Taffy will turn whiter as it is pulled and will get stiffer and harder to pull out. Once it gets white enough, pull the taffy out into long ropes and lay on wax paper. You can twist this rope if you like. Cut the ropes of pulled taffy into bite size pieces with a sharp knife or kitchen shears. If it lasts long enough, taffy can be wrapped in wax paper or plastic wrap and the ends twisted to store.

Brownies

2 cups sugar
$^1/_2$ cup butter or margarine
1 cup nut meats
4 eggs
1 cup all purpose flour
1 teaspoon vanilla
4 ounces unsweetened chocolate
$^1/_4$ teaspoon salt

In a large mixing bowl, beat until light eggs and salt. Add sifted sugar gradually. Continue to beat until light and fluffy. Melt butter and chocolate and fold into eggs. Add vanilla and flour. Beat until smooth. Fold in nuts. Grease and flour a 9 x 13 inch pan. Pour in the batter and bake for 30 minutes at 350 degrees. When cold, cut into squares.

Our birthday cake—we all took turns posing with it.

Chocolate Dreams

1 cup shortening
2 cups sugar
1 teaspoon vanilla
$^1/_2$ teaspoon salt

4 squares unsweetened chocolate
4 eggs (well beaten)
1-$^1/_4$ cups sifted flour
1 cup chopped walnuts

Melt chocolate and shortening in upper part of double boiler over water. Add sugar and mix well. Stir in eggs and vanilla. Add flour and salt, mixing thoroughly after each addition. Remove from heat. Add chopped nuts. Spread in well-greased three quart pan (13-$^1/_2$ x 8-$^3/_4$ inch). Bake about 18 minutes at 400 degrees. Cool.

Peanut Butter Cookies

$^1/_4$ pound butter or margarine
1 cup milk
2 teaspoons vanilla
1-$^1/_2$ cups quick oatmeal

1 cup brown sugar
13 ounces peanut butter
pinch salt

In a medium saucepan, bring butter, sugar and milk to a boil. Boil for 2 minutes and add peanut butter, vanilla, and salt. Stir until well blended. Add oatmeal and stir. When cooled slightly, drop by tablespoon on wax paper.

Aunt Sue's Peanut Butter Fudge

2 cups sugar
6 tablespoons butter
1 teaspoon vanilla
1 cup peanut butter (smooth or chunky)
1 cup half and half (or $^2/_3$ cup milk)
1 7-ounce jar marshmallow cream

Combine sugar, milk, and butter in a saucepan. Bring to boil over medium heat stirring constantly. Cook to 234 degrees or soft ball stage on candy thermometer.

Remove from heat and stir in marshmallow cream and vanilla. Beat well. Stir in peanut butter. When smooth and blended, spread evenly into buttered 8 inch square pan. Optional: $^1/_2$ cup of melted semi-sweet chocolate pieces can be added at the last minute and swirled into the fudge.

My nieces, Dena, Donna, Chris, and Jennifer at the Hat House for Jennifer's bridal shower.

Sallie Messer's Fudge

4 cups sugar
3 tablespoons cocoa
pinch of salt
1 teaspoon vanilla
2 cups cream
$^3/_4$ cup Karo syrup
$^1/_4$ pound butter

Cook all ingredients over medium heat in a medium saucepan to the soft ball stage on a candy thermometer. Remove from heat. Place pan in a bowl of cold water and beat until thick. Pour into a buttered pan to cool.

Date and Nut Balls

2 cups chopped dates
2 cups sugar
4 cups Rice Krispies cereal
1 cup coconut
2 eggs
$^1/_2$ cup margarine
2 cups chopped nuts

In a large saucepan, bring the eggs, sugar, margarine, and dates to a boil. Boil for 9 minutes; remove from heat and add the chopped nuts and Rice Krispies. After cooled, form into balls the size of a walnut and roll in coconut.

Gingerbread

1 cup sugar
1 cup molasses
1 egg
2 teaspoons baking soda
2-$^1/_2$ cups flour
1 teaspoon ginger
1 teaspoon cinnamon
dash salt
1-$^1/_2$ cups boiling water
$^3/_4$ cups shortening or butter

In a mixing bowl, cream butter or shortening and sugar. Add one beaten egg and molasses. Beat well. Sift flour and spices and mix well with the butter mixture. Add the boiling water in which the soda has been dissolved. The batter will be very thin. Bake in a 350 degree oven until done. about 30 minutes.

Jim and Jon Hager of Hee Haw fame. I think I'm dancing with Jon, but I don't know, maybe it's Jim.

Favorite Sugar Cookies

Mama always makes a lard can full of these for Christmas. Some of them get decorated with bright-colored sugars and sparkles and some are left plain to be enjoyed with a cup of hot coffee or spicy holiday tea. They never last long enough but always seem to taste better the longer they are in the lard can.

4 cups flour
4 cups granulated sugar
4 eggs
1 pound butter (absolutely butter)
1 teaspoon vanilla

In a large mixing bowl, combine flour, sugar, melted butter, eggs, and vanilla and mix well together to make dough. Refrigerate 2–3 hours or overnight. Roll out small amounts on floured board. You may have to knead some more flour into the dough to make it roll easily. Cut in desired shapes with cookie cutter. Bake at 375 degrees about 10–12 minutes.

Orange Carrot Cookies

1 cup shortening
$^3/_4$ cup sugar
$^1/_4$ teaspoon salt
1 egg
2 cups flour
2 teaspoons baking powder
3 tablespoons orange juice
1 jar strained carrots baby food
1 teaspoon vanilla
powdered sugar

Cream sugar and shortening. Add egg and orange juice. Add salt, flour, and baking powder. Add carrots and vanilla. Bake at 400 degrees for 12 minutes. Ice with powdered sugar.

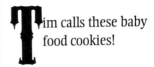

Tim calls these baby food cookies!

Me, Dolly, and Mario Ferris at Mario's Italian Restaurant for Dolly's birthday party.

Anabel's Raisin Slice Drops

Helen gave me this recipe, one of her favorites.

2 cups raisins
1 cup water
1 cup shortening
2 cups sugar
3 eggs (beat well)
1 teaspoon vanilla
1 cup chopped nuts (optional)
4 cups flour
1 teaspoon baking powder
1 teaspoon baking soda
2 teaspoons salt
$1 \cdot 1/2$ teaspoons cinnamon
$1/4$ teaspoon nutmeg
$1/4$ teaspoon allspice
$1/8$ teaspoon cloves

Add water to raisins and boil for 5 minutes, then allow to cool. Cream shortening and sugar. Add eggs and beat well. Add vanilla and the cooled raisins to mixture. Add chopped nuts and stir well. In another large mixing bowl, sift flour with baking powder, baking soda, salt, cinnamon, nutmeg, allspice, and cloves. Add to raisin mixture. Bake at 350 degrees 15–18 minutes.

Pecan Balls

1 cup soft margarine
2-1/4 cups flour
1/2 cup powdered sugar
1 teaspoon vanilla
1/4 teaspoon salt
1 cup finely chopped pecans
2 tablespoons cream

In a large mixing bowl, gradually add powdered sugar to margarine and cream. Add vanilla, flour, salt and chopped pecans. Blend well. Chill 2–3 hours. Shape into small balls about the size of marbles. Place on greased cookie sheet. Bake at 350 degrees for 15–18 minutes. Remove from pan and roll hot cookies in powdered sugar. Cool and roll again in powdered sugar.

These are a bit sweet, but if you have a sweet tooth, you'll love 'em.

"Uncle Sam" gone country fashion.

Ranger Cookies

Tim's favorite on a cold and rainy day. Mine, too!

2 cups flour
1 cup white sugar
1 cup brown sugar
$^1/_2$ teaspoon salt
1-$^1/_2$ teaspoons baking powder
1 teaspoon baking soda
1 cup vegetable oil or safflower oil
2 eggs
1 teaspoon vanilla
2 cups Wheaties cereal
1 cup grated coconut

In a large mixing bowl, sift together flour, white sugar, brown sugar, salt, baking soda, and baking powder. Add shortening, eggs, and vanilla. Mix well. Add Wheaties cereal and coconut and mix well again. Drop by spoonfuls onto greased cookie sheet. Bake at 350 degrees for 15–18 minutes.

Mince Meat Cookies

3 cups flour
1-$^1/_2$ cups sugar
$^3/_4$ cup butter flavored Crisco
3 well-beaten eggs
1 teaspoon baking soda
$^3/_4$ teaspoon salt
1 19-ounce jar condensed mince meat or
$\quad$ $^3/_4$ cup prepared mince (add 3
$\quad$ tablespoons water if condensed
$\quad$ mince meat is used)
1 cup chopped walnuts

Cream Crisco, sugar, and eggs. Combine flour to creamed mixture using only half of the flour at this time. Add salt, baking soda, mince meat, walnuts, and remaining flour to mixture. Drop from teaspoon onto greased pan. Bake at 350 degrees 10–15 minutes.

Try at your own risk. I take no responsibilities for your weight gain …

No Bake Cookies

We used to have these in grammar school. I love these cookies almost as much as I did the meat loaf at Caton's Chapel Grammar School.

2 cups sugar
$^{1}/_{2}$ cup evaporated milk
3 tablespoons cocoa
$^{1}/_{2}$ cup peanut butter
1 teaspoon vanilla
3 cups quick oatmeal

Bring sugar, milk, and cocoa to a boil. Add peanut butter. Stir until melted. Add vanilla. Stir in quick oatmeal. Drop by spoon on wax paper. Cool and eat.

Tim, Mom in a mumu, and me at a Luau in Hawaii.

Yummy Cookies

1 cup butter or margarine
2 eggs
$^1/_2$ teaspoon salt
2 tablespoons water
1 cup moist coconut
1 cup chopped nuts

1-$^1/_2$ cups brown sugar
2-$^3/_4$ cups flour
1 teaspoon baking powder
1 teaspoon vanilla
6-$^1/_2$ ounces pitted dates

Combine all ingredients in a large mixing bowl. Drop by teaspoon onto a slightly greased cookie sheet. Bake 8 to 10 minutes at 350 degrees.

Peanut Butter Cookies

1 cup brown sugar
1 cup margarine
2 eggs
1-$^1/_2$ teaspoons soda
1 cup white sugar
1 cup peanut butter
2-$^1/_2$ cups flour
1 teaspoon vanilla

Sift flour. Combine all ingredients. Drop by teaspoon onto a greased cookie sheet and bake 8 to 10 minutes at 350 degrees.

Corn Flakes No Bake Cookies

I like anything with peanut butter. Kids love helping you make this one.

1 cup white corn syrup
1 cup sugar
1 cup peanut butter
6 cups Corn Flakes cereal

In saucepan, add corn syrup and sugar. Bring to a boil, stir well. Add peanut butter, stir until dissolved completely. In large bowl, pour mixture over six cups Corn Flakes. Place by tablespoon onto wax paper to cool.

My brothers, Floyd and Randy, at Floyd's party for his hit song "Rockin' Years."

FISH

When many, many moons have passed, and your little ones have gone out into the world to live their lives and you are left at home, use this book to cook your fish, and (fondly we hope) recall their fourth grade years.

Most of these fish recipes came from a book that Tim made for me when he was in that grade. I have used these many times and I still treasure his little drawings in the book.

Me, Willadeene, Cassie, and Rachel recording in the studio for Dolly's Christmas special.

Mama's Salmon Patties

2 eggs, beaten
1 small chopped onion
salt and pepper
4 tablespoons flour, plain
1 15-ounce can salmon (do not drain)

In a large mixing bowl, mix all ingredients into a stiff batter. Drop batter by heaping table-spoons into hot oil and fry until brown on both sides.

When I cook, I have a certain menu in mind. For example, I always serve mashed potatoes, green peas, cole slaw, hot yeast bread, and iced tea with salmon patties.

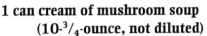

Broccoli Tuna Roll Ups

1 can cream of mushroom soup
   (10-^{3}/$_4$-ounce, not diluted)
1 10-ounce package frozen broccoli
   (thawed, drained, cut in 1-inch
   pieces) or 2-^{1}/$_2$ cups fresh broccoli
1 cup shredded Cheddar cheese
1 cup milk
1 can tuna, drained (10 ounces)
6 small flour tortillas
1 tomato, chopped
1 can french fried onions (3 ounces)

Combine soup and milk in a mixing bowl; set aside. Combine tuna, broccoli, ^{1}/$_2$ cup cheese, and ^{1}/$_2$ can onion rings. Stir in ^{3}/$_4$ cup soup mixture. Divide tuna mixture evenly between tortillas and roll up. Place seam side down in a lightly greased 9 x 13 inch baking dish. Stir tomato into remaining soup and pour over top of tortillas.

Bake covered at 350 degrees for 35 minutes. Top center of tortillas with remaining cheese and onions and bake uncovered 5 minutes longer.

Dolly and Carl caught cuddling near the food in Rachel's kitchen.

Baked Flounder with Mushrooms

2 pounds fresh or frozen flounder filets
2 tablespoons lemon juice
6 tablespoons butter or margarine
$^1/_2$ cup dry cooking sherry
1 6-ounce can mushrooms, drained
6 tablespoons Parmesan cheese
1 can clear chicken broth (13-$^3/_4$–ounce)
$^1/_2$ cup flour
2 cups half and half
6 tablespoons Corn Flakes cereal
lemon slices, parsley for garnish

In a large skillet, combine fish, chicken broth, and lemon juice. Heat to boiling, lower heat, and simmer 20 minutes or until fish is done or flakes easily. Drain fish, reserve 1 cup liquid.

Divide fish. Put in a casserole. Melt butter in a saucepan. Stir flour into butter gradually. Add half and half and sherry. Stir in reserved liquid. Cook over low heat, stirring constantly until sauce bubbles and thickens. Add mushrooms. Season to taste with salt and pepper. Pour sauce over fish. Mix Corn Flakes and cheese. Sprinkle over top of fish. Bake 350 degrees for 30 to 35 minutes and garnish with lemon slices and parsley.

Stella Parton's Country Cookin'

Tuna Fish Croquettes

2 cans tuna
1-$^1/_2$ cups cracker meal
1 egg
1 package mashed potatoes
1 onion, chopped

Drain cans of tuna. Empty package of mashed potatoes into a saucepan and follow directions. Mix tuna, mashed potatoes, onions, and egg together in large bowl. Shape tuna into size you prefer croquettes to be. Roll croquettes in cracker meal. Put into hot grease. Cook until brown.

Tuna for Two Noodle Casserole

2 envelopes Lipton Cream of Mushroom Cup-A-Soup
1 3-$^1/_2$ ounce can tuna, drained and flaked
1-$^1/_4$ cups boiling water
1-$^1/_2$ cups cooked noodles ($^1/_4$ of 8-ounce package)
$^1/_2$ cup cooked peas

In a one quart casserole, combine soup with water. Fold in noodles, tuna, and peas. Bake 20 minutes at 375 degrees.

Tuna Pie

2 9 inch pie crusts
$^1/_2$ cup peas
2 small boiled potatoes
1 family size can tuna
$^1/_2$ cup carrots
1 cup white sauce

Mix all ingredients, add salt and pepper to taste. Put in crust and top with another crust. Bake at 400 degrees for 45 minutes.

Chopstick Tuna

1 family size can tuna
$^1/_2$ cup milk
2 cups diced celery
1 cup salted split cashew nuts
2 cans mushroom soup
2 large cans chow mein noodles
1 cup green onions, chopped
1 can mandarin oranges, drained

Mix together the above ingredients, with the exception of the oranges. Cook in oven at 375 degrees for 15 to 20 minutes. After baking, top with mandarin oranges. Put the orange sections on just before serving.

Tuna Salad Bake

1 can cream of chicken soup
¹/₄ cup finely chopped onion
¹/₂ teaspoon salt
1 6-¹/₂–ounce can tuna, drained
    and flaked

1 cup celery, diced
¹/₂ cup mayonnaise
dash pepper
3 hard boiled eggs, sliced
1 cup crushed potato chips

Combine all ingredients (except chips) in a large mixing bowl. Turn into 1-¹/₂ quart casserole. Sprinkle crushed potato chips on top. Bake for 35 minutes at 400 degrees. Makes 6 servings.

Tuna Fish à la King

1-¹/₄ cups canned tuna fish
¹/₃ teaspoon salt
1 cup milk
1 tablespoon butter
2 tablespoons canned pimentos
2 tablespoons flour
crumbs

Flake tuna and add pimentos, cut fine. Add butter and salt and allow them to heat thoroughly. Add milk into which the flour has been dissolved and cook until smooth and creamy. Pour into buttered baking dish, dot with butter and crumbs and brown quickly in hot oven (400 degrees). Serves 4.

Blushing Tuna Pie

3 6-$^1/_2$–ounce cans tuna, drained
    (reserve liquid)
$^1/_2$ teaspoon salt
$^1/_4$ teaspoon pepper
1 cup shredded Cheddar cheese (sharp)
$^2/_3$ cup ketchup
2 tablespoons flour
1-$^1/_2$ cups milk
$^1/_2$ teaspoon Worcestershire sauce
1 unbaked 9-inch pie shell
parsley

Mix tuna, ketchup, and salt in a bowl. Put
reserved tuna oil into a saucepan. Blend in
flour and pepper, heating until bubbly.
Gradually add the milk, stirring constantly.
Bring to boil. Cook 1 to 2 minutes. Remove
from heat. Add the cheese and stir until melted. Add the Worcestershire sauce and tuna.
Mix well. Pour into shell. Bake at 400 degrees
30 to 35 minutes or until pastry is golden
brown and mixture is bubbly. Remove from
oven and sprinkle lightly with snipped parsley.
Serves 4.

Tuna Fish Avocado Casserole

2 cans tuna fish
4 tablespoons flour
1-$^1/_2$ cups milk
salt and pepper
cracker crumbs
4 tablespoons butter or margarine
2 teaspoons mustard
$^1/_2$ cup light cream
1 avocado, peeled and diced

Drain tuna fish fine. Melt butter or margarine in double boiler and blend with flour and mustard. Add milk and cream. Cook over hot water, stirring constantly until smooth and thickened. Add tuna. Season to taste with salt and pepper. Remove from heat. Fold in avocado. Fill casserole with alternate layers of cracker crumbs and tuna fish mixture, ending with crumbs. Dot with butter or margarine. Bake at 400 degrees until mixture begins to bubble. Serve at once. Serves 6.

My little sister, Cassie, and my little brother, Randy, hiding Easter eggs for the children at the Tennessee Mountain Home.

Kidney Bean and Tuna Salad

2 cans (1 pound each) red or
    white kidney beans,
    rinsed and drained
3 scallions, chopped
1 teaspoon salt
1 can (7 ounces) tuna, drained
    and broken into large
    pieces

$^1/_4$ cup wine vinegar
$^1/_4$ cup chopped parsley
$^1/_4$ cup salad oil
dash pepper
2 hard boiled eggs
lettuce leaves

Mix ingredients (except eggs) and place on lettuce leaves. Garnish with eggs.

Shrimp with Cheese Sauce

2 cups milk
3 tablespoons butter
1 tablespoon Worcestershire
    sauce
dash red pepper (optional)

2 tablespoons flour
1 cup grated Cheddar cheese
$^1/_2$ teaspoon prepared mustard
1 teaspoon salt
1 cup shrimp, cooked

Mix milk, flour, and butter together in a sauce pan for 3 minutes. Add
remaining ingredients. Simmer until shrimp turns white and add grated
cheese (approximately 12 to 15 minutes). Pour over rice and serve.

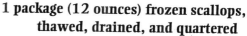

Seafood Coquilles

1 package (12 ounces) frozen scallops, thawed, drained, and quartered
1 can (6 ounces) sliced mushrooms, drained
1 tablespoon grated lemon peel
1 tablespoon chopped chives
1 package (10 ounces) frozen cooked shrimp, thawed
2 cans (10 ounces) condensed cream of shrimp soup
grated Parmesan cheese or french fried onion rings

Heat oven to 400 degrees. Mix all ingredients except cheese. Place about 1 cup mixture in each of 5 or 6 baking shells. Place shells on baking sheet. Bake 15 minutes. Remove from oven, top shells with cheese, and bake for 2 to 3 minutes longer. Makes 5 to 6 servings.

My niece, Heidi Lou's singing debut at the Hat House opening. She's Randy's daughter.

Quiche aux Crevettes (Shrimp Quiche)

1 cup cooked and shelled shrimp
2 tablespoons butter
tarragon
$^1/_2$ cup grated Swiss cheese
1-$^1/_4$ cups milk
1 8-inch partially cooked pie shell
$^1/_3$ cup dry white vermouth
salt and pepper
1 tablespoon tomato paste
$^1/_4$ cup grated Cheddar cheese
3 eggs
nutmeg

Toss shrimp for two minutes in hot butter, over
medium heat. Season with salt, pepper, and
herbs; add vermouth and boil rapidly. Spread
in bottom of shell. Beat together eggs, milk,
pepper, and nutmeg. Add tomato paste. Pour
over shrimp. Spread cheese on top. Dot with
butter. Bake approximately 20 minutes at
350 degrees until done.

Barbecued Shrimp

1 clove garlic, pressed
$^1/_2$ teaspoon salt
$^1/_2$ cup salad oil
$^1/_4$ cup soy sauce
$^1/_2$ cup lemon juice
3 tablespoons finely chopped parsley
2 tablespoons finely chopped onion
$^1/_2$ teaspoon pepper
2 pounds large shrimp, peeled

Combine first 8 ingredients to make marinade. Mix well. Place shrimp in a shallow dish, add marinade. Cover and refrigerate 2 to 3 hours. Thread shrimp onto cocktail skewers. Broil or grill over medium heat about 3 to 4 minutes on each side. Serve with cocktail picks. Yields 15 to 20.

My nieces Hannah, Rebecca, and me trying to figure out a chocolate cake.

Shrimp Creole

³/₄ cup bacon fat
3 large onions
2 cans tomato paste
4 or 5 pounds cooked shrimp
1 tablespoon garlic salt
1 tablespoon flour, if needed to thicken
2 bell peppers
1 cup celery
2 cans water
1 tablespoon vinegar
2 tablespoons chili powder
1 can green peas
salt to taste

Melt the bacon fat in a large heavy skillet. Add the chopped onions, peas, celery, pepper, garlic salt. Cook on high heat for about 3 or 4 minutes. Add the water, tomato paste, chili powder. Simmer another 10 minutes on low heat (covered). If this needs to thicken, place 1 tablespoon of butter in a small sauce pan to melt. Slowly add flour until dissolved (usually about 5 to 6 minutes on medium heat). Add this to the other mixture. Boil shrimp in water or vinegar in covered kettle until the shrimp are pink. Cool, peel, rinse. Add to above mixture, cover and simmer 10 minutes. Serve over rice.

My son Tim, about 3 years old, sampling some of my fried chicken. I don't know about those shoes.

Delicious Shrimp Curry

2 $^3/_4$ pound bags frozen shrimp
4 tablespoons flour
1 teaspoon salt
1 tablespoon curry powder

4 tablespoons butter
2 cups milk
6 tablespoons ketchup
1 teaspoon paprika

Cook shrimp according to package directions and drain. Set aside. Melt butter in saucepan over low heat. Stir in flour until smooth. Stir in milk. Add salt, ketchup, curry powder, and paprika. Cook over very low heat for 10 minutes, stirring frequently. Lastly, stir in cooked shrimp and simmer 5 minutes more. For a special touch, pass small bowls of 2 or 3 of the following: chopped peanuts, chopped eggs, raisins, chutney, chopped apples, or chopped onions

Creamed Salmon

1 pound can red or pink salmon
3 teaspoons minced parsley or
2 tablespoons chopped sweet pickle
2 cups medium white sauce

Drain salmon. Remove skin and bones. Flake coarsely and fold salmon and juice into white sauce in top of double boiler. Continue cooking over boiling water until thoroughly heated. Add minced parsley or pickle, if desired, just before serving. Makes 5 servings.

Salmon Soufflé

2 tablespoons butter or margarine, melted
2 cans (16 ounces) red Salmon, drained
    and flaked
2 tablespoons minced onion
1 teaspoon salt
paprika
$^1/_2$ cup milk
4 slices bread, torn into pieces
2 eggs, separated
3 tablespoons lemon juice
$^1/_2$ teaspoon pepper

Mix butter, milk, and bread. Stir in salmon, egg
yolks, lemon juice, onion, salt, and pepper.
Beat egg whites until stiff. Fold into salmon
mixture. Pour ingredients into greased 1-$^1/_2$
quart casserole. Sprinkle with paprika. Bake
uncovered 1 hour.

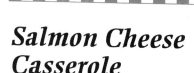

Salmon Cheese Casserole

1 can pink salmon, bones removed
2 pieces chopped toast
1 teaspoon lemon juice
dash salt and pepper
1 stick butter
2 eggs
$^3/_4$ cup grated American cheese
$^1/_2$ cup milk

Melt butter in casserole. Mix all ingredients in large mixing bowl, then place in casserole dish. Bake at 350 degrees for about 30 minutes.

Salmon Loaf

2 cups cooked salmon
$^1/_2$ cup soft bread crumbs
salt and pepper
2 eggs, beaten
$^1/_4$ cup butter, melted
1 tablespoon minced parsley

Flake salmon and add beaten eggs. Add remaining ingredients. Place in greased loaf pan. Bake at 350 degrees for 40 minutes. Serve with egg sauce. Serves 4.

Salmon Patties

1 can of salmon
$^1/_3$ cup chopped onions
1 tablespoon cornmeal
2 eggs
1 tablespoon flour
salt and pepper to taste

Combine all ingredients (except meal) and make into patties. Preheat cooking oil 300 to 350 degrees. Dip salmon patties into the meal and fry until golden brown.

Salmon Croquettes

1 small can salmon
$^1/_4$ teaspoon baking powder
$^1/_4$ cup onion, grated
2 tablespoons mashed or diced potatoes

Mix all ingredients well in bowl. Beat one egg. Have ready about 1 cup cracker crumbs. Make 6 balls of salmon. Dip in egg, roll in crumbs, and fry in hot oil or Crisco. Turn until all sides are browned. Place on paper towel, then on serving plate.

Salmon Cheese Loaf

2 cups flaked, cooked, or canned salmon
3 tablespoons milk
$^1/_2$ teaspoon salt
cracker or bread crumbs to make a stiff mixture
1-$^1/_2$ cups grated cheese
1 egg, well beaten
1 tablespoon melted butter
few grains pepper

Mix all ingredients. Pack into loaf pan. Cover the top with buttered crumbs. Bake at 375 degrees until golden brown. Serves 6. (For Tuna Cheese Loaf, use tuna in place of salmon.)

Hush Puppies

1-$^1/_2$ cups self-rising corn meal
$^1/_2$ cup flour
1 egg
1 finely chopped onion

$^1/_4$ teaspoon pepper
$^1/_4$ teaspoon salt
1 cup buttermilk

Note: 2 cups cornmeal mix works well in place of the meal and flour.

Mix dry ingredients. Add buttermilk, egg, and onion. Drop by teaspoons into hot shortening, oil, or fat. May be fried in the same pot in which the fish are fried. Remove and drain when they turn a golden brown.

Fried Crab, Italian Style

This recipe is for six crabs, but may be doubled for a large family. Remove backs from crabs, wash well and set aside.

$^1/_2$ cup grated Parmesan cheese
1 teaspoon salt
6 cloves garlic
1 egg
$^1/_2$ teaspoon garlic salt
$^1/_2$ teaspoon pepper
mozzarella cheese
water

Soak the live crab in 1 teaspoon of salt and water for 10 or 12 minutes. Drain and remove backs, wash, and set aside. Cut garlic cloves into small pieces; dice $^1/_4$ of small mozzarella cheese ball. Place garlic clove and one cube of mozzarella cheese into each crab shell. Take crab meat removed from shells and boil 12 to 15 minutes, let cool. Drain and cut into small pieces.Mix crab meat, Parmesan cheese, and pepper. Stuff in shells. Dip stuffed crab into beaten egg. Dip into flour and fry in oil until golden brown.

I tried this—it tastes great!

Crab Spaghetti Casserole

1 9-ounce package spaghetti
3 tablespoons butter
1 cup milk
1-$^1/_2$ cups flaked crab meat
$^1/_3$ teaspoon pepper
1-$^1/_4$ cups cream of mushroom soup (con-
densed)
$^1/_2$ pound sharp American cheese (grated)

Cook spaghetti in boiling salted water until tender. Drain. Heat soup, stirring until smooth. Add butter and milk. When hot, remove from heat and stir in grated cheese, saving some to sprinkle on top. Combine cheese sauce with spaghetti, crab meat, and pepper. Place in greased shallow casserole and sprinkle with remaining cheese. Bake in hot oven (400 degrees) about 30 minutes. Serves 8.

Christmas party at Rachel's house. In our family most special occasions center around food and good fun.

Deviled Crabs

1-¹/₂ pounds crab meat
¹/₄ cup toasted bread crumbs
few drops of garlic juice
1 tablespoon chili sauce

2 hard boiled eggs, grated
1 teaspoon lemon juice
dash of cayenne pepper
mushroom soup to moisten

Mix entire recipe together. Fill shells with mixture and top with bread crumbs and dot with butter. Bake for about 20 minutes or until brown in 350 degree oven. The recipe is quickly made and may be allowed to stand in ice box several hours before cooking.

Night Before Crab Casserole

3 slices bread
1 cup mayonnaise
6 hard boiled eggs, chopped
¹/₂ cup Corn Flakes cereal

2 6-ounce cans crab meat,
   drained
1 cup half and half
1 tablespoon minced onion
¹/₂ teaspoon salt

Take crust off bread and cut bread into cubes. Mix crab, mayonnaise, half and half, eggs, onions, salt, and bread cubes. Place in greased casserole dish and put in refrigerator overnight. An hour before dinner, sprinkle Corn Flake crumbs over top and bake at 350 degrees for 1 hour.

Deviled Crab

1 chopped bell pepper
1 mashed garlic clove
2 stalks chopped celery
4 slices bread (soak in milk
     and squeeze out)
$^1/_3$ cup mayonnaise
1 tablespoon Worcestershire sauce
seasoned salt
Tabasco
1 chopped onion
3 chopped green onions (tops included)
3 tablespoons chopped parsley
$^1/_2$ cup grated sharp cheese
3 cans crabmeat
2 beaten eggs
juice of 1 lemon
pepper

Sauté bell pepper, onion, garlic, green onions, celery, and parsley. Add to the remaining ingredients. Mix well. Fill individual ramekins. Cook in 300 degree oven for 30 to 40 minutes. May be made the day before serving.

Lobster Stew

2-$^1/_2$ cups milk
2 tablespoons butter or margarine
salt and pepper
2 cups light cream
1-$^1/_2$ cups lobster meat
celery salt

Combine milk, cream, and butter. Cook over medium heat, but do not let it come to a boil. Add lobster, salt, pepper, and celery salt. Reduce heat. Simmer.

Drawn Butter Sauce

4 tablespoons butter
1 teaspoon lemon juice
2 tablespoons flour
freshly ground pepper

Melt 2 tablespoons butter; add flour, lemon juice, and pepper until smooth. Add one cup hot water, bring to a boil, stirring constantly. Reduce heat and cook for 5 minutes. Add remaining 2 tablespoons butter and stir until melted.

Hot and Spicy Sauce

$^1/_2$ cup chili sauce
1 tablespoon and $^1/_2$ teaspoon
    lemon juice
$^1/_2$ teaspoon brown sugar
$^1/_4$ teaspoon red pepper sauce
1 small clove garlic, crushed

$^1/_4$ cup chopped onion
1 tablespoon salad oil
1 teaspoon vinegar
$^1/_8$ teaspoon dry mustard
$^1/_8$ teaspoon salt

Heat all ingredients to boiling. Reduce heat, simmer 5 minutes. Makes about $^3/_4$ cup.

Parsley Butter

1 cup butter
2 tablespoons lemon juice
2 tablespoons chopped parsley
freshly ground black pepper

Cream butter. Add remaining ingredients and mix thoroughly. Makes about 1-$^1/_4$ cups.

Fried Cross Lake Catfish

2 8-ounce catfish
yellow corn meal
salt
Milani dill sauce
white corn meal

Dip catfish in milani dill sauce. Roll in mixture of yellow and white corn meal and salt. Put on tray and place in icebox for several hours to set. Drop in deep fat fryer, which is set at 350 degrees, and cook for 10 to 12 minutes, or until golden brown and floats. Serve with tartar sauce, sliced onions, and hush puppies.

Dill Sauce

$^1/_2$ lemon
$^2/_3$ cup mayonnaise
1 tablespoon dill weed
dash of Tabasco sauce

Squeeze juice from fresh lemon into mayonnaise. Add a dash of Tabasco sauce. Add dill weed. Mix together.

Cross Lake has a special catfish, Blue Channel, because the feeding gives special flavor.

Catfish Recipe

2 pounds catfish
2 cups corn meal
1 tablespoon black pepper
3-$^1/_2$ cups shortening
1-$^1/_2$ tablespoons salt
1-$^1/_2$ tablespoons red pepper

Put shortening in the skillet. Let skillet get hot. Mix ingredients. Batter the fish in the ingredients. Fry the fish. After one side is brown, turn over to let the other side brown. Serve with lemon wedges.

Baked Oysters

1 quart oysters and liquid
2 spring onions, chopped
salt and pepper
$^1/_2$ lemon, juice and
    grated peel

6 slices bacon
1 tablespoon chopped parsley
2 tablespoons butter
$^1/_2$ teaspoon gumbo file*
bread crumbs

Arrange ingredients in layers in low buttered casserole: first a layer of chopped raw bacon, then a layer of oysters, then crumbs, parsley, grated lemon peel, chopped onion, gumbo file, lemon juice, then repeat. Pour in oyster liquid. Dot top with butter and bake in a quick oven 400 degrees about 30 minutes. Serves 4.

* A Creole thickener (can use tapioca flour)

Perch or Halibut Steak

1-$^1/_2$ pounds perch or halibut
1-$^1/_2$ teaspoons salt
2 tablespoons chopped onion
$^1/_4$ cup water (for frozen fish)
2 tablespoons butter
dash pepper
1 tablespoon chopped parsley
2 tablespoons flour
$^1/_4$ teaspoon salt

Cut fish into individual servings. Brown the
fish in hot fat in bottom of pressure cooker.
Place fish on rack. Season with salt and pepper. Sprinkle with onions. Add water. Cover,
set control, and cook 4 minutes. Reduce pressure normally. Remove fish and place on hot
platter. Thicken liquid with flour mixed with
cold water. Stir until smooth. Add salt and
parsley.

Scalloped Oysters

1 pint oysters
$^1/_2$ cup butter, melted
$^3/_4$ cup light cream
$^1/_4$ teaspoon Worcestershire sauce
2 cups medium coarse cracker crumbs
    (46 crackers)
$^1/_2$ teaspoon salt

Drain oysters, reserving $^1/_4$ cup liquid. Combine crumbs and butter. Spread a third of crumbs in 8 inch round pan. Cover with half the oysters. Sprinkle with pepper. Using another third of the crumbs spread a second layer. Cover with remaining oysters. Sprinkle with pepper.

Combine cream, reserved oyster liquid, salt, and Worcestershire sauce. Pour over oysters. Top with remaining crumbs. Bake in moderate oven (350 degrees) about 40 minutes or until done. Makes 4 servings.

Rachel and me—a little sister hug.

Oyster Stuffing
for the gourmet palate

3 tablespoons melted margarine or butter
$^1/_2$ cup finely chopped celery
1 teaspoon savory
1 teaspoon salt
1-$^1/_2$ dozen small oysters with liquid (or
    1 cup canned oysters, chopped)
1 teaspoon chopped parsley
$^1/_2$ cup finely chopped onion
1-$^1/_2$ cups day old bread crumbs
1 egg, beaten
$^1/_2$ teaspoon finely grated lemon rind

Heat butter in skillet. Brown onion and celery.
Reduce heat to low and add bread crumbs, seasonings, and egg. Toss to mix thoroughly. Add
oysters with their liquid, lemon rind, and parsley. Cook over low heat about 10 minutes.
Makes about 2 cups.

*Tennessee Governor Ned
McWhorter and me at a benefit
concert in Nashville.*

Stella Parton's Country Cookin'

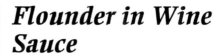

Flounder in Wine Sauce

2 pounds flounder filets
dash pepper
$^1/_2$ teaspoon salt
2 tablespoons melted butter
$^1/_3$ cup dry white wine
chopped parsley
1-$^1/_2$ teaspoons salt
3 sliced tomatoes
2 tablespoons flour
$^1/_2$ cup of milk
$^1/_2$ teaspoon crushed basil

Thaw frozen filets. Skin and sprinkle both sides with salt and pepper. Place filets in a single layer in greased baking dish. Arrange tomatoes over top of filets. Sprinkle tomatoes with salt and pepper. Blend flour into butter and add milk gradually. Stir in wine. Add basil and parsley. Cook until thick and smooth. Pour sauce over top of tomatoes. Bake in moderate oven at 350 degrees for 25 to 30 minutes until fish flakes easily with a fork. Sprinkle with parsley. Serves 6.

Fish Cakes

3 medium potatoes (1 pound)
$^3/_4$ teaspoon salt
$^1/_2$ cup evaporated milk
2 tablespoons flour
1-$^1/_2$ cups water
1 7-ounce can fish flakes
dash pepper
3 tablespoons salad oil

Pare potatoes. Cut in half and turn into
saucepan. Add water and salt. Cover and cook
until tender, about 20 minutes. Turn heat low,
add drained fish flakes, milk, and pepper.
Mash and whip until smooth and stiff. Cool
mixture. Spread flour on waxed paper. Divide
mixture into half cupfuls, dropping into flour.
Shape it into flat cakes. Coat both sides with
flour. Heat oil in heavy skillet until hot, but
not smoking. Lay in cakes and brown richly
on both sides. Serve hot, plain or with tartar
sauce. Serves 5.

*Hannah and me coloring Easter
eggs at her house. She's not too
big on eating them, but she loved
the artwork we came up with.*

PASTA

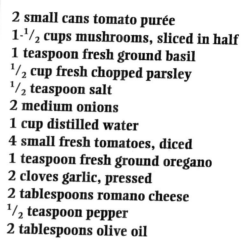

Tomato Sauce

2 small cans tomato purée
1-$^1/_2$ cups mushrooms, sliced in half
1 teaspoon fresh ground basil
$^1/_2$ cup fresh chopped parsley
$^1/_2$ teaspoon salt
2 medium onions
1 cup distilled water
4 small fresh tomatoes, diced
1 teaspoon fresh ground oregano
2 cloves garlic, pressed
2 tablespoons romano cheese
$^1/_2$ teaspoon pepper
2 tablespoons olive oil

Concert stage in Holland '93.

Sauté onions and garlic (use olive oil). Add diced tomatoes and spices. Cook 10 minutes, moderate heat. Add tomato puree and distilled water. Add cheese when sauce has cooked 30 minutes. Add mushrooms; mushrooms are optional. Cover and simmer on low heat about 40 minutes. Sometimes I add a small can of tuna or clams. This is my all-purpose tomato sauce. Then I add whatever I'm in the mood for, like maybe slices of zucchini. It really doesn't matter.

Giuseppe's Tomato Sauce

3 tablespoons oil
4 cloves chopped garlic
1 medium finely chopped onion (4 ounces)
2 stalks finely chopped celery (4 ounces)
1 carrot finely chopped (4 ounces)
1-$^1/_2$ tablespoons Giuseppe's Sauce Seasoning (or Italian seasoning)
1 pound can whole tomatoes
1 15-ounce plain tomato sauce

Put finely chopped onions, celery, carrots, and 4 ounces of water into blender and blend into a purée. If food processor is used, omit water. In a 7 quart pot, add oil and chopped garlic and sauté until golden. Do not overcook. Add puree of onion, celery, and carrots. Stir well for 5 minutes. Add Giuseppe's Sauce Seasoning, or any all-purpose seasoning, and mix well. Add tomatoes with liquid and tomato sauce. Simmer over medium heat 45 minutes and stir often. Cook longer if thicker sauce is desired.

For a heartier, more robust sauce, we recommend adding one ounce porcini mushrooms, which have been soaked for 10 minutes, plus $^1/_2$ pound fresh, sliced mushrooms, and/or one pound ground meat, browned and drained. If adding these extra ingredients, more Giuseppe's Sauce Seasoning may be needed, according to taste.

Bob's Lasagna

1 32-ounce jar of Ragu Extra Thick & Zesty Sauce
1 28-ounce can of Progresso Tomato Purée and tomato paste
4 to 6 fresh diced or quartered tomatoes or 1 32-ounce can of
    whole peeled tomatoes
Tabasco or Louisiana Hot Sauce
2 12-ounce boxes of fresh mushrooms
2 large or 4 to 5 small onions
2 large bulbs of garlic
$^1/_4$–$^1/_2$ cup olive oil
2 boxes of lasagna noodles
ground beef or soy burger
salt and pepper
parsley
grated cheese: mozzarella, ricotta cheese, cottage cheese (optional)

In a large pot, add sauce, puree, and paste. Slowly bring to cooking temperature. Add onions and garlic and cook until tender. Add olive oil, black pepper, and Tabasco sauce or Louisiana Hot Sauce to taste. Add tomatoes and mushrooms and cook covered for about 15 minutes. Stir often to prevent burning on bottom. Salt may be added to taste.

Sautéed ground beef or soy burger may also be added. Beef will make the sauce more greasy and soy burger will tend to thicken the sauce so more oil and some water may be added to get the desired consistency.

In two large pots, cook lasagna noodles as directed. Do not drain, just add cold water. Grease large baking dish. Place a layer of noodles on the bottom. Cover with sauce and ricotta cheese. Here you can add parsley, grated cheese, or slice mozzarella, if you want. Continue working layers until pan is full or sauce and cheese are all gone. Cover with a final layer of lasagna. Now you can freeze it in the pan or prepare it by placing it in a 350 degree oven for about 30 minutes or longer, if frozen.

Aunt Sue's Baked Spaghetti

$^1/_2$ **pound spaghetti**
$^1/_2$ **green pepper (diced)**
1 large can tomatoes
several slices of bacon
1 medium onion (chopped)
Cheddar cheese

In a large pot, cook the spaghetti as directed. Drain. In a skillet, fry bacon and remove when cooled. Sauté green pepper and onion in the bacon grease left in the skillet. Add the drained spaghetti and a large can of tomatoes. Heat all together in the skillet just enough to make sure everything is heated through.

In a baking dish or casserole dish, pour ingredients from the skillet. Dot the top with chunks of Cheddar cheese. Bake at 450 degrees until the cheese melts.

My beautiful sister, Cassie, models 9 to 5 fashions at Rachel's Fashion Show.

Gnocchi
with Tomato Sauce

Sauce

$^1/_2$ pound mushrooms
2 carrots
1 onion
$^1/_2$ tablespoon basil
1 celery
1 tablespoon oregano
2 cloves garlic

3 tablespoons corn oil or margarine
16 ounces water or wine
1 pound tomatoes (cut up)
1 16-ounce can of plain tomato sauce
salt and pepper

Dough

4 pounds potatoes
3 egg yolks

2 pounds flour
salt

In large pot, cook peeled potatoes until soft. Mash. Add flour, salt, and egg yolks. Make dough. Break into link sausage thickness (keep dough floured). Cut into 1 inch pieces. Drop dough pieces into boiling water (Gnocchi) for 3 to 5 minutes or until it floats to top of water.

Chop up carrots, celery, onion, garlic, and mushrooms. Sauté in large skillet with corn oil, margarine for 10 minutes. Add tomato sauce, chopped tomatoes, spices, and water. Simmer for 40 minutes.

SOUPS &
SALADS

Chicken Corn Soup

1 stewing chicken
2 stalks celery (chopped)
1 teaspoon parsley flakes
1 garlic clove
1 bag frozen white corn
1 package fine noodles
salt and pepper to taste
1 medium onion, chopped (optional)

Cook chicken in a large pot until done. Take chicken out of broth. Remove chicken from the bones. Cut into small pieces and put back into broth. Do not pour fat out! Add celery, parsley flakes, garlic clove, onion, salt, and pepper and cook until celery is done. Add noodles and corn last, amount to your liking. Cook until tender, approximately 7 to 10 minutes. Serve hot.

Grandpa Parton, Dolly, and Grandpa Owens at the first Dolly Parton Day in Sevierville, Tennessee.

Slum Gullion

4–6 potatoes (1 potato per person)
3–4 slices lean bacon
1 large onion
flour

Peel potatoes and cut into chunks (about $^1/_8$ inch thick). Put in a pan and cover with water. Dice a large onion and add to the potatoes. Add 3 to 4 slices of lean bacon to the same pan. Bring this to a boil and cook until potatoes and bacon are well cooked. There should be water left in the pan. Thicken this with flour to make a gravy. Serve over biscuits.

S lum Gullion is supposed to be a poor man's stew, but wealthy is he who has feasted on Mom's Slum Gullion served on her "made from scratch" biscuits.

Judy's
Calico Bean Mix*

1 pound barley pearls
1 pound dried black beans
1 pound dried red beans
1 pound dried pinto beans
1 pound dried navy beans
1 pound dried lentils
1 pound dried great northern beans
1 pound dried split peas
1 pound dried black eyed peas

Combine all beans. Divide into 2 cup packages for gift giving. Makes 10. Also looks pretty in a large glass jar sitting on kitchen counter. Don't forget to include the soup recipe with the bean mix.

* Use Calico Bean Soup Recipe (see page 146).

Calico Bean Soup

2 cups Calico bean mix*
2 quarts water
1 pound ham, diced (optional)
1 large onion, chopped
1 clove garlic, minced
$^1/_2$–$^3/_4$ teaspoon salt
1 1-pound can tomatoes, chopped with
    juice
1 10-ounce can tomatoes and green
    chiles (or substitute another small
    can tomatoes and 1 small can
    green chiles)

Sort and wash 2 cups bean mix. Place in large
soup pot, cover with water 2 inches above
beans and soak over night. Drain beans, add
2 quarts water and the next 4 ingredients.
Cover and bring to a boil. Reduce heat and
simmer 1-$^1/_2$ hours or until beans are tender.
Add remaining ingredients, simmer 30 minutes, stirring occasionally. Yield 8 cups.

* See recipe on page 145.

Salad

1 large can crushed pineapple
2 3-ounce packages cream cheese
cup chopped celery
pinch salt
1 package lemon Jell-O
1 4-ounce can chopped pimento
$^1/_2$ cup chopped nuts
1 cup whipping cream, whipped

Drain pineapple. In a saucepan, boil Jell-O and two cups of water. Chill until syrupy. Mix cream cheese, pimento, salt, celery, and nuts together. Add to Jell-O. Add pineapple and fold in whipped cream.

Kidney Bean Salad

2 cans kidney beans (drained and washed)
2 hard boiled eggs (cut up)
$^1/_2$ cup celery (chopped)
1 small onion (chopped)
1 green pepper (chopped)
1 small sweet chopped pickle

In a small bowl, mix. Toss with Italian dressing.

Orange Jell-O Salad

2 3-ounce boxes orange Jell-O
1 6-ounce can frozen orange juice
1 large can crushed pineapple
2 cups boiling water
1 small can Mandarin oranges (drained)

Dissolve Jell-O in boiling water in mixing bowl.
Add frozen orange juice, drained oranges, and
crushed pineapple. Pour into 13 x 9 inch cake
pan. Refrigerate until well set (several hours).

Topping

1 package Cool Whip
2 cups cold milk
1 3-ounce box coconut cream
instant pudding

In a small mixing bowl, whip together until
thick. Spread on Jell-O.

The youngest Mad Hatter.

Stella Parton's Country Cookin'

Bean Salad

1 can green beans (2 cups)
1 can lima beans
4 tablespoons instant minced onion or
   $^1/_2$ cup fresh onion
1 can wax beans
1 can kidney beans
1 green pepper (diced)

Drain beans and mix all ingredients together in large mixing bowl. Marinate at least 2 hours or overnight in:

$^2/_3$ cup salad oil
$^1/_4$ cup lemon juice
$^1/_2$ teaspoon dry mustard
2 packages dry herb dressing mix
$^1/_4$ cup vinegar
1 tablespoon prepared mustard
$^1/_4$ cup sugar

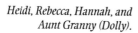

*Heidi, Rebecca, Hannah, and
Aunt Granny (Dolly).*

Cauliflower Salad

1 head lettuce (shredded)
1 pound bacon, cooked and crumbled
1 cup mayonnaise
grated Parmesan cheese
1 head cauliflower (broken up)
1 box frozen peas or mixed vegetables
1 package Good Seasons Italian Mild Dressing Mix

Put ingredients except the last in a large bowl in the order given. Cover with Saran Wrap. Put a dinner plate on top. Refrigerate 24 hours. Toss before serving. Sprinkle the Good Seasons Italian Dressing Mix on top.

The Union Salad

1 package lime Jell-O
$^1/_2$ cup mayonnaise or salad
    dressing
1 cup diced celery
2 tablespoons minced onion

1-$^1/_2$ cups hot water
1 cup cottage cheese
$^1/_2$ cup diced green pepper
stuffed olives or pimentos

In a mixing bowl, dissolve Jell-O and water. Stir in mayonnaise. Cool. Add cottage cheese, diced celery, diced green pepper, and minced onion. Add olives or pimentos. If recipe is doubled, do not double onion and green pepper.

Peach Party Salad

16 marshmallows cut in 8ths
1 pound creamed cottage cheese
$^1/_4$ cup toasted coconut
1 pint sugared raspberries
3 tablespoons raspberry juice
$^1/_4$ cup cream (whipped)
12 peach halves

Soak marshmallows in fruit juice in small bowl. Blend with cottage cheese, whipped cream, and coconut in larger bowl. Add raspberries and mix together. Spoon into peach halves. Serving suggestion: serve with nut bread sandwiches. Extra raspberries can be spooned over the top. Makes 12.

Cabbage or Kraut Salad

1 large can sauerkraut (drained and rinsed)
1 medium onion (chopped)
$^1/_4$ cup oil
$^1/_3$ cup sugar
1 green pepper (chopped)
1 cup celery (chopped)
2 tablespoons pimento or small jar
$^1/_2$ cup vinegar (cider)
1 teaspoon salt

In a saucepan, bring ingredients to just below a boil. Do not boil.

Best Egg Salad Ever

1 hard boiled egg (diced)
$^1/_3$ cup cottage cheese
onion powder
1 green pepper (chopped)
salt and pepper
lettuce

Mix all ingredients in a small bowl. Serve on toast.

Potato Salad

6–10 boiled potatoes (peeled
    and sliced)
$^1/_2$ cup scallions (chopped)
$^1/_2$ cup radish (chopped)
1 cup Italian dressing

3 eggs, hard boiled
$^1/_2$ cup celery (chopped)
1 cup Miracle Whip
paprika

In a large, long dish, slice potatoes. Pour Wish Bone dressing over to coat. Add green onion with tops and toss lightly. Refrigerate for 2 hours. In a small bowl, add chopped eggs, celery, radishes, and Miracle Whip. Mix. Add this mixture to the potatoes. Garnish with paprika.

Tomato Salad Supreme

8 firm, ripe tomatoes (peeled)
1 clove garlic (crushed)
1 teaspoon sugar
$^{1}/_{4}$ cup olive oil
2 teaspoons prepared mustard
$^{1}/_{4}$ cup parsley
$^{1}/_{2}$ teaspoon salt
$^{1}/_{4}$ teaspoon pepper
2 teaspoons cider vinegar

Cut out stems from tomatoes. Slice each one crosswise ($^{1}/_{2}$ inch slices). Form into tomato shape. Place in shallow serving dish. Combine remaining ingredients in small jar. Cover and shake. Pour over tomatoes. Cover tightly and let stand at room temperature for 20 minutes before serving.

Earlene Teaster presenting me with the Key to the City of Pigeon Forge, Tennessee, at the official "Hat House" opening.

Banana-Pineapple Salad

2 packages lemon Jell-O
16 marshmallows (large)
2 bananas
4 cups boiling water
2-$^1/_2$ cups crushed pineapple (drain and
    save juice)

In a large mixing bowl, dissolve marshmallows
and Jell-O in boiling water. When slightly
thickened, add bananas and pineapple. Place
in refrigerator to set.

Topping

2 teaspoons butter
3 teaspoons flour
pineapple juice
$^1/_2$ cup sugar
2 eggs (well beaten)

In mixing bowl, beat ingredients. Spread on
top of chilled Jell-O.

Cranberry Salad

1 pound cranberries
$^1/_2$ pound marshmallows (32)
$^1/_2$ pint cream (whipped)
1 cup sugar
$^1/_2$ pound grapes

Drain cranberries well. Grind cranberries. In a large bowl, mix cranberries, sugar, and marshmallows (cut rather small). Seed and quarter the grapes. Add whipped cream. Mix. Let stand in refrigerator for several hours. Serves 16 to 18.

7-up Salad

2 packages lemon Jell-O
2 whole oranges
2 bottles 7-up
2 cups hot applesauce
juice of 2 oranges

In a mixing bowl, combine Jell-O, applesauce, 7-up, and grind two whole oranges and juice of two others. Chill until ready to serve.

VEGETABLES

Potato Salad

6 medium potatoes
3 stalks parsley, chopped
2 shakes of spike
1 tablespoon mustard
1 teaspoon pickle relish
1 onion
1 teaspoon oregano
dash basil
1 tablespoon mayonnaise

Boil, peel, and dice potatoes. Peel and dice onion. Mix all ingredients in large bowl. Chill until ready to serve.

Hot Potato Salad

6 medium potatoes
1 teaspoon sugar
$^1/_2$ tablespoon salt
$^1/_2$ teaspoon pepper
1 tablespoon vegetable oil

1 medium onion
1 teaspoon vinegar
1 tablespoon water
1 tablespoon mustard

Boil potatoes. Let cool. Peel and dice in medium chunks in large bowl. Peel and dice onion (fine). Mix sugar, water, vinegar, oil, salt, and pepper. Heat until sugar dissolves. Add mustard. Stir mixture into potatoes and onions until mixed well. Serve warm.

Eggplant

4 fresh medium egg plants
1 cup milk
1 cup flour
3 eggs
salt and pepper

Peel and slice eggplant. Salt and pepper on both sides. Dip in egg and milk mixture. Roll in flour on both sides. Brown on each side in hot oil until brown and tender. Let drain on paper towel. Layer with tomato sauce and Parmesan cheese. Bake in oven at 400 degrees until bubbly. Can also be used instead of meat in lasagna. Serves 6.

Italian Bell Peppers

6 large bell peppers
   (3 red, 3 green)
1 tablespoon safflower oil

4 garlic cloves
1 tablespoon olive oil
$^1/_4$ teaspoon sea salt

Preheat oven to 400 degrees. Wash peppers. Roast on oven rack turning until skin turns brown on all sides. Don't overcook—watch carefully. Remove from oven. Let cool. Peel and clean peppers. Tear into strips. Dry on paper towel on both sides. Slice garlic cloves. Add oil and salt to peeled peppers in a medium bowl. Stir to coat well. Cover and let stand overnight in mixture. Serve with bread. Eat as finger sandwiches or pocket bread. Keeps well in refrigerator for several days.

Cabbage Strudel

Dough

$^1/_2$ teaspoon salt
1 egg
1 tablespoon melted butter

6–8 tablespoons water
1-$^1/_2$ cup all-purpose flour

Cabbage Filling

4–5 tablespoons bacon
    drippings*
1 medium head cabbage
    (shredded)
$^1/_2$ teaspoon salt

$^1/_4$ cup chopped sweet red pep-
    per (green pepper also)
$^1/_8$ teaspoon black pepper
1 teaspoon Hungarian paprika
$^1/_4$ cup chopped onion

Sift flour and salt onto a bread board. Make a well in the center. In a small bowl, combine egg, butter, and 6 tablespoons of water. Pour into the well. Begin kneading from center outward and continue until dough is smooth. Do not add additional water unless needed to make dough stick together. Roll the dough out as thin as possible into a rectangle on a floured tea towel and brush with additional melted butter. Cover and let rest for 30 minutes.

Heat bacon drippings in an iron skillet and put in the shredded cabbage. Stir and add chopped onions, salt, and sweet red pepper. Cover and cook over low heat for 15 minutes, stirring to prevent burning. Add pepper and paprika last, stir into mixture, remove from heat, and let cool completely.

Spread cabbage mixture over dough, roll up with edge of tea towel, and place on oiled baking sheet. Brush with melted butter and prick with a fork to allow steam to escape.

Bake 375 degrees for 30 minutes or until golden brown. Yields 4 to 6 servings.

*variations: Cooked pork, chicken, sausage, or bacon can be added.

Baked Onions

$^1/_3$ **cup honey**
$^1/_2$ **teaspoon salt**
$^1/_4$ **cup butter**
6 large onions (sliced)
$^1/_2$ **cup black walnuts**

Preheat oven to 425 degrees. In a small saucepan, heat butter, honey, and salt. In a greased 13 x 9 inch baking dish, arrange onions. Pour honey butter mixture evenly over onions. Add walnuts last 10 minutes of baking. Bake 45 minutes or until onions are fork tender and golden brown. Makes 6 to 8 servings.

This recipe came from a local grocery store. It's easy to make. I serve it with mashed potatoes.

Escallop Corn

1 can cream style corn (or 1 can whole kernel corn, add $^1/_2$ cup milk*)
$^1/_4$ cup margarine or butter

crushed crackers
paprika
salt and pepper

Butter bottom and sides of a casserole dish. Pour corn into a mixing bowl with crushed crackers to thicken corn mixture. Pour into buttered dish, dot with margarine or butter, sprinkle paprika, and salt and pepper to taste.

Bake uncovered in 400 degree oven for 20–25 minutes.

*canned milk is good

Breaded Tomatoes

1 can tomatoes (3 people per 1 can)
margarine
1 to 1-$^1/_2$ slices of bread
pinch of sugar

In a mixing bowl, break up bread. Add tomatoes, sugar, and margarine. Put mixture in a buttered pan, dot with butter, and bake at 400 degrees until bubbly, about 15 minutes.

Scalloped Potatoes

**4 medium potatoes
1 cup shredded Cheddar cheese
1 small can condensed milk
2 medium onions
1 stick butter**

Peel and slice potatoes and onions. Place in buttered casserole dish, alternating potatoes, onions, and cheese. Pour over milk and add cheese and remaining butter. Sprinkle with paprika. Bake in oven at 400 degrees about 30 minutes until bubbly and brown on sides. Serves 6.

Nieces Jennifer and Donna, sisters Cassie, Dolly, and Rachel, younger nieces Hannah, Rebecca, and Heidi, and Aunt Dorothy Jo at Dolly's TV taping.

Afterword

Having gone over the recipes for this cookbook, I realized that many of them were passed along to me by family and friends. They naturally assumed I would know what they meant by phrases such as "till its done", "dancing in the pan", or "jest a dab". If I didn't have the foggiest notion what they meant, I would call or write to say "I tried out your recipe last night on company—what was that little extra something you did to yours that tasted so much better than mine?" If I pleaded sweetly and bragged big enough, I could usually persuade them to give me that last secret ingredient. As my friend Darlene would say, "It's what you don't say that counts; that's the country way." Therefore, if you try these recipes and can't figure out something, feel free to stop me the next time you see me. I'll be glad to go over the directions with you.

My mom always says that good cooking not only requires a great recipe but also the freshest ingredients available and a bushel of creativity. Of course, the fresher the ingredients, the better the flavor. For example, I learned to churn and make fresh butter when I was about twelve years old. I also picked black berries and made jelly. I don't think there is anything better than one of mama's hot "cathead" biscuits with homemade butter and jelly for a late breakfast, even today.

Professional chefs are very precise about their recipes with the intention that other cooks will follow them exactly; it's almost like a science. In contrast, the country cook comes up with a good dish and can't remember how much of an ingredient they put in to make it taste so good. Sometimes a dish is borne out of a cook's mood or what was available in the kitchen at the time. If you are lucky enough to become known for a particular creation among your family and friends, they may not be above trying to weasel the recipe out of you, and stealing your thunder at the next family reunion or holiday get together. In my family, cooking is a game of competition and the best cooks are secretive about their recipes. That's why this cookbook is so special— it's filled with family secrets dating back to my great grandmother's time.

In fact, I've been told that my great grandmother's favorite saying was "the way to a man's heart is through his stomach." I recently had a unique experience that made me believe that wise old adage. A couple of years ago I took a trip to Tampa, Florida to promote my first cookbook and food products on the Home Shopping Network. One evening my agent and I walked into a restaurant at our hotel. To our great surprise and delight, there sat Omar Sharif at a table having dinner with two of his managers. By coincidence, we were given a table right next to them. We overheard one of the managers say, "that's the lady the Network gave your Limo to at the airport this morning. I think she's here to promote her cookbook." Immediately he got up from his seat, came over, and charmingly introduced himself, insisting we join them. Of course, we couldn't be rude and decline dinner with Dr. Zhivago, could we? He began extolling the virtues of women who were good cooks. He said he always found them to have loving hearts and to be generous with their friends, and that they were especially capable of bringing out great passion in their husbands, In his sexy Egyptian accent, he invited me to give him a call next time I visited

Paris—France. He added that he would be happy to take me to the best restaurant in the city. Of course, I was very flattered and amazed at the attention he showered on me throughout dinner, all because of my little ole cookbook. Needless to say, I floated back to Nashville and made everything I could think of using curry—curry pudding, curry cake, curry casserole, curry pie—the list was endless and I almost had a new cookbook on my hands. All the while I was playing Lara's theme. You can bet your best pair of cowgirl boots, I'll be ready to impress him the next time our paths cross out here on the road. Hopefully, you get the idea. Now just let the competition begin and I'll see you in my next volume of Country Cookin'.

Index

Stella Parton's International Fan Club
P. O. Box 120295
Nashville, TN 37212